DIANE VON FURSTENBERG

with

Linda Bird Francke

SIMON & SCHUSTER

D I A N E

A SIGNATURE LIFE

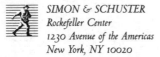

SIMON & SCHUSTER
Rockefeller Center
1230 Avenue of the Americas
New York, NY 10020

10 9 8 7 6 5 4 3 2 1

Library of Congress Cataloging-in-Publication Data

Von Furstenberg, Diane.
 Diane : a signature life / Diane von Furstenberg,
with Linda Bird Francke.
 p. cm.
 Includes index.
 1. Von Furstenberg, Diane. 2. Women fashion
designers—United States—Biography. I. Francke,
Linda Bird. II. Title.
TT505.V66V66 1998
746.9'2'092—dc21
 [b] 98-42511 CIP
ISBN 0-684-84383-8 (hc.)

AUTHOR'S NOTE
AND
ACKNOWLEDGMENTS

MY CLOSE FRIENDS and family often reproach me that I never tell them much about what I do. I remember my friend Jane Wenner teasing me that I can be more personal selling on television than when I speak to her on the phone. It is a bit exaggerated, but I see what she means. I don't really like to discuss what I do or even how I feel, yet here I am opening my life and revealing so much of myself in this book. Why this contradiction of being so open publicly while reserved privately? I don't know how to answer this question, but I feel obligated to raise it. Through the process of writing this business memoir I have tried to define myself to myself, retrace my journey, my search for freedom, and explain my need to express it through my work. I have tried to be as honest and as lucid as I possibly can; to look back and see how the seeds I planted have evolved in order to garden some more.

This book is mostly about the adventures of my professional life, but because my professional life is so linked to me personally, I have opened many of my private doors as well. However, while I write about the people that have touched my life in significant ways, I have tried to respect their privacy in this book, just as I do in life.

Through anecdotes and sometimes trivial descrip-

tions, I revisited a myriad of landscapes, events, and encounters that tell the story and the adventures of a signature. I have tried to express my feelings of happiness, frustration, and even despair. If I don't dwell on the unhappy feelings, it is because that is my process. In all circumstances, I always look for the light and build around it, with little memory of pain. Often I don't remember if I got to places by design or by adapting to situations. While it is true that I want people to like the book and even me, more important is that I hope this book inspires those who read it.

I want to thank Linda Bird Francke for agreeing to do this book with me. She wrote one of the first stories about Egon and me for *New York* magazine in 1973 and, three years later, my *Newsweek* cover story. Both stories had a major impact on my life. Twenty years later I went looking for her.

Without her, I probably would have never done the book. I also want to thank Alice Mayhew, my editor, for supporting it with such enthusiasm; Elizabeth Stein for her great efforts to bring it to fruition; Jennifer Crawford for her wonderful work making sense of the photographs; Ruth Patkin for helping me to position it; Liza Hemme, my assistant, for her fantastic discretion and efficiency; and my agent, Andrew Wylie, for including me on his list of prestigious clients; David Seidner for photographing me for the cover. All of them gave me the confidence to do the book and constantly reassured me that it was interesting, fun, and—I hope—worthwhile. I want to acknowledge all the people who have worked with me all these years and have given me support with their enthusiasm and belief.

I want to thank my children for making me so proud

to be their mother and my own mother for having given me the courage to love life with passion. Finally, I want to thank Barry for being Barry and everyone who has entered my heart for making me realize how large and expandable it is.

TO EGON,

who gave me
the children and the name

CONTENTS

You cannot kill time
without injuring eternity.

—Henry D. Thoreau

BIRTH PAINS

THE LIGHT IS BRIGHT, too bright, in the fitting room at Saks. My reflection in the mirror looks horrible to me as I peer over a young woman's shoulder and show her how to tie my new wrap dress. Twenty-five years have passed since I was first in that fitting room at Saks, looking into the same mirror but over the shoulder of her mother, using the same gestures and the same responses, wrapping the same dress. "Tight. You've got to pull it really tight," I instruct the young woman of today before moving on to the customer in the next fitting room. "Now see how pretty and sexy you look?"

It is just after noon on September 9, 1997, and the dress department on the seventh floor of Saks Fifth Avenue in New York looks less like the launch of a new collection than the premiere of a long-awaited movie. Television cables from CBS and ABC snake through the racks of the new silk wraps. Fashion reporters from *The New York Times*, *Women's Wear Daily*, and *Vogue* are interviewing the multitudes of customers, a few of whom are wearing original dresses from the 1970s. The rebirth of my dresses has surpassed expectations.

On the one hand, I am thrilled. Salespeople are combing the racks with telephone orders, just as they did twenty-five years ago. Customers of all ages are grabbing two

or three dresses at a time. We've already sold out of the dress with the signature pattern as well as the new bamboo print.

"It feels like déjà vu," I say over and over to the press, wishing I weren't so tired, wishing they weren't taking my picture. "It's great to be back."

As much as I am thrilled with the moment, I feel like a bullet train that has left the station before the itinerary is drawn. The response to the launches at Saks in Portland, San Francisco, Cleveland, St. Louis, Houston, and Boston has been so astonishing that we have had to cancel the events in Chicago and Atlanta because we've run out of dresses. I'm already late on designing the next collection for spring and summer, and the phones at my new headquarters, when they work, are ringing constantly with orders from stores in England, France, Canada, Japan, and Sweden.

All of this is good news, but I'm not ready. I don't have a business plan or a strategy in place, nor do I have a president to manage the new company. We've only just moved my new headquarters into the old carriage house in Greenwich Village, and I'm still figuring out how to design it. There aren't enough phone lines, so the computers keep breaking down. I am distracted and exhausted.

ESTABLISHING A BUSINESS was not new to me. In the last two decades I have launched with great success a dress business, a cosmetics and fragrance company, a home furnishings business, a licensing business, a couture collection, and, during the five years I lived in Paris, a publishing company. Since my return from Paris in 1990, I have ventured into the television

shopping business and made a lucrative design deal. But this moment at Saks was particularly exhilarating.

Saks is one of the top-tier specialty stores in the country and exactly where I wanted my new line, *DIANE*, to be. I just never thought it would happen so fast—and, on top of it all, with the dresses. Only the year before, I had been negotiating my return to the retail world after a ten-year absence with Federated Department Stores, the huge consortium that includes Bloomingdale's, Macy's, Rich's in Atlanta, and Burdine's in Florida. We were not talking dresses then but an array of products including sportswear, intimate apparel, accessories, and home furnishings, which the Federated stores would carry under my name as a private-label brand exclusive to them. A wide range of products bearing my name had generated sales of well over $1 billion in the 1970s and early 1980s, and there was reason to believe that the new brand could build up the same volume.

The deal had begun to fray amid grumblings from a few Federated buyers and managers that my name was no longer "valid" and was too "old" for the young customers the department stores wanted to attract. We had countered the charges by inviting the skeptics to the office to show them new designs, and we thought we had convinced them all. But obviously we hadn't.

I was devastated when the deal collapsed at the eleventh hour in the summer of 1996. But the rejection proved to be a blessing. Because I had not been able to convince the doubters, I decided to reposition the brand's image on my own: I would go back to the original product that had launched me in the first place, the dress.

DIANE THE DRESS, a simple cotton knit wrap I'd designed more than twenty years before, had found its way into almost every closet in America and had become a symbol of the era. The dress in its many colorful signature prints had achieved such popularity that in the five years or so the wrap dress was on the market, I sold more than five million of them.

The demand for the wrap had returned in the 1990s along with the fashion nostalgia for the 1970s. A whole new generation of hip young women in their twenties was snapping up the original dresses for up to $200 in vintage shops. There was even a waiting list, which I found amusing at first but intriguing enough to pay attention to. Actress Kelly Lynch told me she'd bought two of them. My twenty-five-year-old daughter, Tatiana, who is always ahead of her time, was wearing them, as were many of her friends, and scouring the vintage stores for more.

The whole fashion industry was copying the look. Sometimes it made me smile, sometimes not. When one young designer, Todd Oldham, invited me to his fashion show to "pay homage" to Diane Von Furstenberg, part of me was flattered—but another part felt like saying, "Wait a minute. I'm not dead yet."

Though I had sold my original dress company in 1978 and my beauty business in 1983, and the licensed products bearing my name had gradually disappeared from the stores by the late 1980s, the name Diane Von Furstenberg still ranked number seven in designer name recognition in a 1993 Fairchild Publications poll published in *Women's Wear Daily*. It was ridiculous, really. But not taking advantage of

the name recognition and the demand for the product that had made it would have been even more ridiculous, I thought.

By 1997, I was in a better position to bring back the dresses, in fact, than I had been when I introduced them in the 1970s. Brand names were now far more important in fashion marketing. You no longer bought a pair of jeans but Calvin Klein jeans. Suits had become Armani; shoes, Manolo Blahnik or Christian Louboutin or Chanel. Image sold. "You see this shoe?" a buyer at Barneys New York told a shoe designer friend of mine. "If it has one CC [for Coco Chanel] on it, it will sell twice as many as a plain shoe. If it has two CCs on it, it will sell twice as much. With four CCs, it will sell four times as much."

Chanel was just one of the old brands currently riding the wave of success. Gucci, which had descended into tackiness, became hot again in the 1990s with the great talent of designer Tom Ford, who created a modern product and a new image. Tom, whom I greatly admire, was just one of the designers who had been urging me to revitalize my own brand. "I'm a fan of yours, and I really think you should make your dresses again," he had said to me at a cocktail party. If one has gained brand recognition, it's very hard to take it away.

I WENT TO PARIS for the fashion shows soon after the collapse of the Federated deal in 1996. I was still feeling disappointed and angry, but I was also somewhat relieved because I had really wanted to reintroduce my brand at specialty stores rather than department stores. The kind of woman I wanted

to reconnect with was far more likely to buy her clothes at a boutique or in Saks Fifth Avenue or Neiman Marcus than at a midlevel department store. And it was in Paris that I ran into Rosemarie Bravo, the president of Saks.

"Diane, we need your dresses" were the first words out of her mouth. "All these designers are showing dresses with your spirit. We need you."

I didn't wait to blink. "Who is your buyer? I may have something for you," I told her.

The buyer immediately came to the office when I returned to New York. I showed her the concept for the new line, *DIANE,* and the disappointment of the last eighteen months with Federated suddenly evaporated. "We want the dresses, absolutely," she said. "How soon can we have them?"

LIGHT POURS through the glass atrium on the roof of the old, four-story carriage house I bought for my new headquarters. I love the new, though unfinished, business space more than I ever anticipated.

There is ample room to incorporate the past, the present, and hopefully the future into this one beautiful building; all the archives, the press books, the designs, old samples and new. I want everybody who walks in to immediately understand the philosophy behind the brand.

The building also symbolizes the integration I've always sought between work and life. It totally reflects who I am. I have incorporated the years I spent in Bali with the Balinese furniture and the carved wooden sculptures I have collected, and my years in Paris by creating a downtown salon.

The idea was to design the space as an ever-changing stage for small presentations, full-fledged fashion shows, and parties. The reception area at the entrance is constructed of four pieces of a Ruhlman staircase of the 1930s I found. The ground floor has the grand piano that used to be in my Fifth Avenue apartment and the Tiffany chandelier that had belonged to Tallulah Bankhead. I love every single element of the building and how together they represent the integration of both my personal taste and my professional identity.

STILL, I HAD MOMENTS of uneasiness as the new line of dresses evolved. As an impulsive girl in the 1970s, I had followed my instincts in marketing and design and achieved considerable success. Were my instincts still valid at fifty? Pragmatist Ronald Lauder tried to reassure me over lunch one day by pointing out that the best years for his mother, Estée Lauder, had been between fifty and eighty. While I found that inspiring, I still wasn't sure.

Old insecurities kept resurfacing. My trust in others to oversee the business side of the companies while I concentrated on design and marketing had resulted in colossal crises over the years. Had I learned from those crises, or was I doomed to repeat them?

I WORRIED about returning to the dresses, which, for all the small changes, were nearly the same as they'd been twenty years ago. I believed the dresses were right for the time, but would they be sneered at by the press, by the fashion industry?

I was somewhat comforted by the reactions of people whose opinions I respect. "Of course it's going to work," Amy Spindler, the knowledgeable young fashion writer for *The New York Times,* told me during a visit to my office to see the new dresses. "You already have an identity, and this is a great product."

Young designers were also enthusiastic about the new dresses, especially the one printed with my actual signature. I had come up with the print idea while talking on the phone and playing around with my signature. I turned it into a pattern, and that was the one that the talented designer Marie-Anne Oudejans chose to wear to a wedding for which she herself had created most of the clothes for the wedding party.

Nothing prepared me, however, for the overwhelming response to the launch.

THE LAUNCH of the new dresses turned out to be a reunion of sorts, nostalgic but without being sentimental, much like women reminiscing about their children. "I'm so happy you're back," women said to me or "I've waited all these years for you" or "I wish I hadn't thrown out your dresses." It was a very nice feeling.

Interestingly, I realized that over the years women have associated me and the dresses with their sexuality. Some brought scrapbooks to the launches, and when they showed me their old photographs and talked about the dresses, they had these little smiles that were full of memories. For me, too, the dress is a benchmark in time. "When I was last here, I had a very little boy," I had told the sales force at Saks Fifth

Avenue the morning of the launch there. "That little boy is now a man, and I am here today with Alexandra, his beautiful wife."

Alexandra's presence was pure pleasure. I'd had no idea when she came to work with me part time in 1996 after she and my then-twenty-five-year-old son, Alexandre, returned from their honeymoon, that she would grow into such an integral part of the company. Alexandra has a great sense of style and a sophisticated eye. She understood that nostalgia for the wrap was one thing, too much retro was another.

We worked together to adapt the old dress to modern taste. The new collars were smaller and rounded rather than pointed and big. We shortened the length of the dress from midcalf to the knee. The new fabric is a silk knit instead of the original cotton jersey. One style of the new wrap was cut very small to hug the young, sexy bodies of Alexandra's generation and the fittest among mine. Another wrap style, with no collar or cuffs, was a more forgiving A-line for women with hips.

IT WAS SCARY how fast the brand was taking off. Because of the launch schedule, I couldn't be at my studio in New York. I had to put on a front in all the stores and be constantly photographed. The stress showed in the pictures. I felt I looked bad, which only added more stress.

Everything I did, everywhere I went highlighted the passage of time and made me feel old. I looked at the pictures the women brought me of themselves in their dresses twenty years earlier, and whether they still looked good or not, they

had changed, and so had I. I felt the same as I had before, doing the same thing in the same cities at the same stores with the same dresses, but time had passed and I saw it as I looked at myself in the fitting room mirrors and in the pictures in the newspapers.

Meanwhile, I needed time to rethink the positioning of the brand. Customer patterns were developing that we hadn't expected. A lot of the women my age who remembered the wrap with such fondness couldn't always wear the new dresses. While that was a bit disappointing, the surprise was their daughters. It was the younger women who were the most excited about the dresses and who were giving me the greatest ego satisfaction. I laughed when Sandra Bernhard, while a guest on a late-night show, declared that "the wrap is back," and I smiled when the beautiful Serena Altschul, the host of *MTV News: Unfiltered*, whom I've known since she was in kindergarten with my daughter, wore the dress on air and called to tell me she was going to wear it again the next day because she loved it so much.

Gwyneth Paltrow, the beautiful young star of the movie based on Jane Austen's *Emma*, was wearing the new dress. So was Raquel Welch's daughter, Tahnee, and Alana and Rod Stewart's daughter—everybody's daughter, it seemed.

It is such an extraordinary and unexpected compliment to be dressing a whole new generation of women. But what will it mean to our positioning and distribution? Will the young shop at Saks? Or will they continue the trend of shopping at boutiques like Scoop, a hot boutique in New York's SoHo, which has continually sold out of the dresses?

□

I had a constant sense of the pressure of time as I traveled from city to city. Every day started at 6 A.M. with morning television appearances, followed by press interviews, breakfast meetings, and talks to the Saks sales personnel before the stores opened, then continued with personal appearances with the customers, more interviews, cocktail receptions, dinners.

"Enjoy it. Just enjoy it," Barry Diller, the pillar of my life, told me when I called him from the road. Barry, a media mogul who was building a new company of his own at the time, was as reassuring as ever. We had been tycoon lovers in the 1970s, he the thirty-something CEO of Paramount Pictures, I the twenty-something fashion entrepreneur. More than twenty years later, we still talked five or six times a day, traveled together, spent holidays and birthdays together, and were partners in business and life. During the launch, Barry lent me his plane as often as he could to make the tour easier for Alexandra and me.

I welcomed the weekends when I could drive to Cloudwalk, my 150-year-old farm in Connecticut. I have a great need for green, for solitude, for the space I have enjoyed there since I bought it in 1974 for my twenty-seventh birthday. I've remained thankful ever since that I had the courage so early on to buy the fifty-eight-acre haven of apple orchards, gardens, and hiking trails along a river. My children grew up at Cloudwalk, as, in a sense, did I. Our dogs are buried there. I will be buried there. The farm has remained the basis of my sanity and the core of my family. No matter

where we are in the world, we always return to Cloudwalk, where we gather at the same kitchen table under the same faded wallpaper.

I knew the work ahead would be intense, but recapturing the professional identity I'd lost in the ten years or so I'd been out of the retail market was vitally important to me. My work and my designs have always been an expression of me and an extension of my personality, and I wanted that identity back.

There was nothing in my personal life to interfere with the workload. The dynamic, in fact, was just the opposite. Often my business efforts and successes have followed personal disappointments, and in 1997 the man who had held a prominent place in my heart for the last few years was going through personal turmoil and slowly withdrawing from me. All the wonderful time I had spent traveling with him, visiting Sri Lanka, the island of serendipity, driving through the deserts of Cappadocia in Turkey and the canyons in Utah, and discovering the treasures of Dresden, lay heavily on my hands now.

I had fewer family demands as well. My children, whom I had basically raised on my own, had blossomed into adults and were happily living their own lives. Tatiana, a writer, was living in Los Angeles and working on her first novel. Alexandre was married and had started his own investment business in New York.

It had been Alexandre's drive and ambition in starting his company, in fact, that had reignited my own. Alexandre was just slightly older than I had been when I'd started my first business, and the more I heard about his plans and saw his excitement, the more envious I became. Just listening

to him made me realize how competitive I am and how much I love and missed designing and selling my own products. I had no idea that my return would be so exhilarating and, at the same time, so frightening.

I turned to my mother, Lily, for reassurance. Her unemotional response to my question "Why am I doing this?" was the same as it has always been: "What would you be doing otherwise?" My mother rarely flatters me and never cautions me. In all my life, she has never said, "It's impossible" or "It's too complicated."

Once again, she encouraged me to move ahead. "Look at what you've accomplished in your life," she said. "You've done it all by yourself, and everyone respects you." To hear her say that went to my heart.

The future of my new business venture was uncertain, but I felt warm and inspired by my mother. Her determination had given me life and shaped my life. I live her lessons every day.

WEAVING
THE FABRIC

LILY NAHMIAS was twenty-one in 1945, when she was freed from the Neustadt-Glewe concentration camp in Germany. She had spent the past fourteen months of her young life being shipped by the Nazis from camp to camp, including Auschwitz-Birkenau and Ravensbrück. She weighed forty-nine pounds, barely more than the weight of her bones alone, when Russian troops liberated the camp, and she was not expected to survive.

She had been arrested in Brussels in the spring of 1944 during a raid in the middle of the night on the house where she was living with a Resistance family who made false papers and arranged transport for Jews. She was taken to the Belgian prison of Malines, where she would be jailed for a week.

People were being arrested and sent to the camps just on the suspicion that they were Jews. "You don't have to say you're Jewish," one of the more sympathetic Belgian guards kept telling her. "Then you won't be sent away."

But she ignored his advice and told prison authorities that she was Jewish. She thought it would be better to be arrested for being Jewish than risk being tortured and forced to expose other members of the Resistance. And then she was loaded onto a train.

□

DIANE MY MOTHER rarely talked about the camps during my child-
hood in Brussels. I remember the numbers that were tattooed
on her arm from two of the three camps she had been in, but
after a while she had the tattoos removed because it annoyed
her to have people constantly remark on them. I don't recall
her ever telling me about the atrocities she had endured.
Sometimes I overheard her talking about it to others, but to
me, if she talked about the camps at all, it was about little
things, such as how much she had longed for a plate of
spaghetti or how she had exchanged a piece of bread for a
comb or how she had cut off the bottom of her dress to
make a belt. They were almost boarding school kinds of
stories, not death camp kinds of stories. She built a defense
out of denial. She often said she had felt her mother's pres-
ence and prayers watching over her during her ordeal of
fourteen months. Somehow she assumed she was going to
survive it all. When her fellow prisoners said, "Do you smell
the crematorium? We're all going to die, we're all going to
die," she chose not to hear them.

 She did, however, tell me the train story many times.
The journey had been a nightmare, of course, especially for
my mother, who had been so protected by her parents that
she had hardly been allowed to even go out by herself and
was now suddenly exposed to so much horror. The days on
the train leading up to the camps seemed to last forever. She
had attached herself to an older woman who spoke a little
German and gave her a sense of protection. My mother
decided never to leave her side.

 Upon arrival at the camp, she stayed close to the

older woman. They stood together when the prisoners were forced to form a long line to await selection. And when the German soldier in charge directed the older woman to join a group on the left, my mother moved quickly with her.

The soldier let her go. It fell to a higher-ranking officer watching the prisoner selection to change the course of my mother's life. Without warning, he grabbed her from the group on the left, hit her with his baton, and threw her into the group being formed on the right. My mother was devastated, unable to comprehend. She had never experienced such hatred for anyone, but in reality that man saved her life. The group on the left was sent to the gas chamber. From this sad event, my mother drew the life lesson that you never really know what's good for you. What may seem to be the absolute worst thing to happen to you can in fact be the best.

What other lesson could be drawn from my mother's recovery from near-fatal starvation, her marriage only six months later to my father, Leon Halfin, who had spent the war in Switzerland, or her courage in ignoring her doctor's life-or-death orders not to get pregnant? I was born on the eve of 1947, the daughter of a survivor, not a victim.

The Holocaust has shaped my character from inception. My birth was a miracle. Had my mother not been pregnant with me, she might not have recovered from her ordeal as determinedly as she did or even survived at all. For her as for many other survivors, coming out of the camps into everyday life was in some ways more difficult than life within the camps. The idealistic vision of the world one has clung to to survive can be shattered when petty realities intrude, when one realizes that people on the outside can also be selfish and insensitive. In fact, my mother talked more

about the disappointment she felt after her return than about the atrocities she had experienced in the camps.

DIANE Ours was not a religious household. I knew I was Jewish, of course, but religion played no role in my childhood. We celebrated Christian holidays, such as the Belgian holiday of Saint Nicolas. After the war, many Jewish people didn't practice their religion. Their memories of the Holocaust were too fresh and painful, the price paid too high. In 1996, I understood completely why Madeleine Albright, the U.S. secretary of state, did not know that some of her relatives had died at Auschwitz. A whole generation had protected their families by keeping their history secret or by denying, as my mother had, the magnitude of the horror. She remained relentlessly positive. She chose to dispel the cold she had suffered walking for days in the snow from camp to camp in the winter of 1945 by buying a sable coat with her reparation check from the German government.

As A CHILD in Brussels, my days were long and boring, and the persistent rain made my curly black hair frizzy and uncontrollable. I hated the fact that my school friends had straight blond hair and I didn't. People thought I was a boy. Others would tell me I was lucky because I wouldn't need to have a perm when I grew up. But I didn't want to have a perm, I wanted to have straight blond hair and to be pretty.

It took me a long time to realize that my childhood feelings of plainness and sometimes even ugliness actually gave me an advantage. The girls who were unanimously considered beautiful often rested on their beauty alone. I felt I had to do things, to be intelligent and develop a personality

in order to be seen as attractive. By the time I realized that maybe I wasn't plain and might even possibly be pretty, I had already trained myself to be a little more interesting and informed.

As a small child I immersed myself in books, trading places with the characters of the Comtesse de Ségur. My mother added poetry, insisting that I memorize and recite to her the seventeenth-century fables of La Fontaine, such as "Le Corbeau et le Renard" and "La Cigale et la Fourmi." She was a young mother, and until I was about eight she treated me like her toy, alternately playing with me and torturing me with her demands. I was relieved when my brother, Philippe, was born and she lost a little interest in me, although I still feared her a lot.

The arrival of Philippe, who is six years younger than I, was doubly important to my life because he awakened my own maternal instincts. I became like a little mother to him. Years later, when my own infant son would cry and wake me in the night, I would instinctively call, "Philippe, Philippe," mistaking him for my baby brother.

I didn't particularly enjoy being a child, though my childhood was perfectly happy. I wanted to be older than I was and never liked people who patronized me because I was a child. I never played with toys or dolls. When I wasn't reading, I was talking to myself in the mirror and pretending I was in the theater. I played make-believe, but it was some-how always about playing real life. I couldn't wait to grow up. After my own children were born, I would always make a point of treating them with respect as individuals and encouraging them to grow up within the realities of the world.

My mother always pushed me toward independence

and freedom, perhaps because of her loss of both in the concentration camps. "Help thyself; Heaven will help thee," La Fontaine wrote. When I was eight years old, she put me on a train by myself to go to Paris, where I was met by my aunt Mathilde. I loved the adventure. When my parents traveled and took me with them, they would go out in the evenings and leave me alone at the hotel. I would sneak out of the room and go talk with the maids and the hotel porters and have a wonderful time. I loved the illusion of having my own separate life.

We traveled a lot, which I loved because it broke the monotony of Brussels. Traveling, just moving around, was a way of life for us. To me it still is. Nothing makes me happier than to discover new countries and lose myself in an unfamiliar landscape where no one knows who I am or where I am. On the road is where I feel the freest and learn the most.

My parents were both immigrants. My mother was born in Salonika, Greece, and moved to Belgium at the age of three. My father was born in Kishinev, Russia (Moldova now, Bessarabia then), and moved to Belgium at seventeen to go to university. After the war he went into the electronics business and became a major European distributor of electronic tubes, a pioneering role my brother would continue when he took over the business, and became an early global trader of cutting-edge semiconductors.

My mother helped my father in business with her strategic mind, but she was never physically strong enough to work. She was so frail she never even worked in our home. Her stamina had been sapped by malnutrition and forced labor in the camps. One of her work details had been to

make bullets in the Krupp arms factory, though she insists that in fact she committed sabotage by only pretending to make bullets.

I loved my father, perhaps more than my mother at first. She was very strict, while he was generous and affectionate. He had unbelievable energy and was always on the road and working with great enthusiasm. With him, everything was quantity and abundance. He loved to buy food, for example, and he would go to France and fill his blue American convertible with crates of tomatoes, peaches, oranges, and other fruits. When you got into his car, you inevitably sat on an apple.

My father was a very forceful man with a huge appetite for life. He always did what he wanted to do, even when it verged on rudeness. In keeping with his Middle European heritage, he would often sing loudly at parties and break glasses. He was very strong with lots of energy, a characteristic I inherited, while from my mother I inherited a more cerebral strength.

Just before I turned thirteen, my mother sent me away to boarding school in Switzerland. My father didn't really want me to leave Brussels, but she insisted that I needed to expand my life experience by going to school abroad. It turned out that my mother had a boyfriend in Switzerland with whom she would later live for twenty years, but I didn't know that then. I was just thrilled to get out of Belgium.

In Brussels, my best friend had been Mireille, one of the straight-haired blond girls. Our favorite game, playing princess, would become reality when Mireille eloped at the age of seventeen with Prince Christian von Hannover, brother of Queen Frederika of Greece and grandson of the

kaiser, and I married a German prince whose title dates from the Holy Roman Empire. At the Pensionnat Cuche, a tiny private school on top of a hill in Lausanne, Switzerland, my best friend was Isabel, a slightly older, sophisticated Venezuelan girl who smoked cigarettes, wore makeup, taught me how to French kiss, and introduced me to Oscar Wilde. I'm not sure that's what my mother had had in mind, but I was finally and happily on my way to starting my own life. And then there was a short and very unpleasant detour.

My parents brought me home to Brussels after two years in Switzerland. Not only was I back to the gray routine but my parents were not getting along and there was a lot of tension in the house. When my parents finally decided to separate, I welcomed it. In keeping with my mother's philosophy of turning negatives into positives, the separation meant that once again my life held the possibility of adventure.

I was thrilled when, the next year, I was sent at the age of fifteen to boarding school in England. There were many foreigners like me at Stroud Court, learning to speak English and preparing for their "O" level exams. It was a very small school and would have a great impact on my life.

Because Stroud Court was a boarding school, there were lots of rules. Some students found the atmosphere restrictive, but I found it liberating. As opposed to living at home, there was not as much attention focused on you as an individual. We all lived under the same rules, and within that framework, I was free. Though it seems silly now, I remember the exquisite feeling of freedom I had during our scheduled "time off"—Wednesdays between noon and 10 P.M. and all day Saturday. That sense of freedom I first experienced in England has probably given me the most pleasure throughout

my life. I get that same feeling now when I steal time from my schedule and do something I'm not supposed to do. I also feel that lightness and happiness in nature.

Stroud Court was a half hour from Oxford in the beautiful English countryside. In periods of unhappiness, generated mostly by my parents' tears and sorrow over their divorce, I would take walks by myself under the trees along the river and feel better with every step.

My parents' generation was more interested in urban life. We had lived in the city, and they relaxed by going to the movies and sitting in cafés. Luckily for me, we had lived near a beautiful forest, and often Mireille and I had walked her dog, Caramel, through the woods, and dreamed of our future lives. It was in England, however, struck by the beauty of nature, that I realized how much I felt it and needed it. When I bought Cloudwalk on a rainy day only twelve years later, it would be largely because of the trees I could see through the car windows and the river rimming the lawn. I gave the startled agent a deposit of $10,000 without even walking the grounds and never regretted it.

The prints for my dresses would draw from nature —the motion of leaves, the ripples on the river, the ancient stones in English walls. At boarding school I started a life-long habit of keeping a journal, and I recorded everything I saw with a camera. In later years, my collection of photographs would often become the basis of many of my prints. I would photograph a fern, for example, and transform the image into an abstract polka-dot pattern.

The profusion of lavender in England would also reappear in my work, but as a favorite scent in my bath and beauty products. All the flowerpots around the pool and in

my studio at Cloudwalk are filled with lavender, a word that comes from *lavare* in Latin and means "to cleanse." Europeans often have lavender in their houses. I believe the scent is therapeutic. I often take a sprig of fresh lavender, crush it between my fingers, and inhale the fragrance.

It never occurred to me as a schoolgirl in England that I would go into the beauty or fashion business. I had no idea what I would do. Because I read so much, one of my friends suggested I become a librarian, but the librarian at the school was an old spinster with big thick glasses. I remember the moments of despair when I was sixteen and thought that I would never find anything I wanted to do. But the seeds were being planted.

I studied beauty that first year in England through the eyes and feelings of Keats. I would never have chosen beauty as a subject, but because that was one of his major topics, I ended up doing my papers about beauty. His "A thing of beauty is a joy forever" and "Beauty is what beauty does" would become my leitmotifs.

I became a romantic in England, imitating Keats, embracing love and the sensual. I discovered physical love, first with a handsome Persian boy named Sohrab who was studying architecture and then, in my second year, with a French girl, Deanna. Both relationships were full of love, hope, and support during the difficult period after my parents' separation. As many divorcing parents do, my mother and father used me as a messenger to each other, and though I pretended I didn't mind, it hurt. I remember how loving Sohrab was and how he took me to an Indian restaurant in Oxford and forced me to eat.

Since those school years in England, I have always,

somehow, been in love, sought love, given love. To me, life is love is life is love. I put those words on a T-shirt later, the words forming a heart. I have written hundreds of love letters, and I have meant every word I wrote. I have tried to save every letter I've received, especially from my children. I also have all the letters my parents wrote to each other during the war and the German occupation before my mother was arrested, which are marked with a thick vertical blue line from the censors, indicating they've been cleared. There is an especially moving one from my mother's sister to my father in Switzerland, telling him, in code, that my mother had been arrested. "Lily has been hospitalized and we are praying for her," my aunt Juliette wrote.

The world we inherited as teenagers would be far less cruel twenty years later. In Europe as in America, the 1960s were a time of social upheaval, of youthful irreverence for the past and a claim on the future. We listened to the Beatles and the Rolling Stones at school and dressed in the "revolutionary" clothes of the era. Once a term we would go to London to shop on King's Road at Biba's or at Mary Quant and bring back the new miniskirts, headbands, and plastic boots that were democratizing fashion and liberating the women who wore them. We felt released from the conventions of our parents' generation and empowered by our own.

Many of us were caught up in the political unrest sweeping postwar Europe as the Communists cemented their hold on the Eastern European countries. I had been somewhat politicized as a nine-year-old girl during the suppression of the 1956 uprising in Hungary by Soviet troops and tanks. My father had volunteered to meet the refugees flood-

ing into Belgium, and he sometimes took me with him when he escorted them from the train station to refugee centers. He was always sensitive to refugees, probably because he himself had been one.

My political education would continue in Spain, where I went in 1965 to study Spanish at the University of Madrid. Spain was under the waning control of General Francisco Franco, the Fascist dictator who had seized the government in 1939 after three years of civil war. There were a lot of riots in Madrid led by students pressing for more cultural and political freedom, as well as illegal strikes called by workers. I didn't study very much because the university was always on strike. I learned Spanish mostly by going to the movies in the afternoon.

I identified with the anti-Franco movement, but more out of anticonformity than political knowledge. I had a vivid sense of the civil war, in which nearly one million people had died—the streets were filled with blind and injured old people—and as a student of the university I could not help being involved in the student protests. There were many churches near the girls' pension where I lived in a grim little room with Deanna, my school girlfriend from England, and I often had to take refuge in them from the violence on the street. I was infuriated during one riot when the police confiscated and ripped up the film in my camera.

My year in Spain was a lonely one. Deanna and I had no social life whatsoever. The only acquaintance I made was with a young man I met in the cafeteria at the Faculty of Philosophy who was very, very angry at Franco and eloquent about his ideas of constructive socialism for Spain. I think, though I'm not 100 percent sure, that his name was Felipe

González Márquez, the man who would become prime minister of Spain in 1982 after leading his Spanish Workers Socialist Party to electoral victory. His newspaper photographs look like the student I had known as Felipe González, who used to write me letters full of anger toward the Franco regime.

It was during my year in Madrid, however, that my life changed. Over the Christmas break I went to Gstaad in the Swiss Alps with my mother and her boyfriend, Hans, and ran into Isabel, the Venezuelan girl I'd known at school in Switzerland. Just as she'd introduced me to Oscar Wilde and cosmetics in school, in Gstaad she introduced me to the jet set.

In contrast to the austerity of my life in Madrid, all of a sudden I was in the midst of all these people who all seemed to know one another and to be effortlessly beautiful and rich. The actress Natalie Wood was part of the group. So was Vladi, a colossal Venezuelan man of Yugoslav origin who fell in love with me and gave me my first silk Emilio Pucci shirt. The print was bold in all shades of green with "Emilio" handwritten all over it. I felt glamorous for the first time in my life. When I went back to my grim little room in Madrid to finish my academic year, I realized that I had moved on. I'd had a little peek into a world that seemed so much fun and I wanted to be part of it. Later, the prints for my dresses would be very Pucci-like.

I WAS LIVING with my mother and her boyfriend after returning from Madrid, dividing my time between the University of Geneva, secretarial school, and a part-time job as a receptionist at Bernie Kornfeld's finance company, IOS.

I was eighteen, and for the first time in my life, I felt my life was exciting. My mother and her boyfriend traveled a lot, and when they were away I could pretend their apartment was my apartment. I even faked appendicitis because I was not prepared for exams, and I convinced the doctor that I had to have my appendix removed. After the surgery, I checked myself into a Swiss clinic with a sunny garden to recuperate. By the time my mother returned from South America, worried about my health, I looked tanned and felt great.

I met Egon later that year at a nightclub in Geneva named Griffin. I wasn't particularly attracted to this handsome blond young man, whose proper German name and title were Prince Eduard Egon von und zu Fürstenberg. He was at school in Lausanne at the time, and I found him a bit childish. Besides, there were lots of other young, good-looking guys in cosmopolitan Geneva and at the university.

My feelings toward Egon began to change on an afternoon ski trip we took together to Megève, an hour and a half outside Geneva. The car got stuck in the snow, and Egon went for help. It turned out to be very easy to get the car out, but I was charmed by Egon's helplessness. I felt a lot of tenderness for him after that, and we became involved. His mother, Clara Agnelli, whose family owns Fiat, had a chalet in Cortina d'Ampezzo, and Egon invited me there for the Christmas holidays. That New Year's Eve, I turned nineteen. I was with him again in Cortina d'Ampezzo for my twentieth birthday. And then I left Geneva for Paris.

I wasn't thinking of marrying Egon, even though I was very much in love with him. Perhaps I was afraid, having

seen the emotional toll that the failure of my parents' marriage had taken. Perhaps my mother's insistence on my personal freedom and independence had translated into an aversion toward dependency of any kind. Or perhaps we were simply too young. In any event, I was determined to create my own life. Egon and I went our separate ways when I took my first professional step as an assistant to a photographer and filmmaker's agent in Paris.

The excitement had started. I was twenty in Paris, working for the agent who represented all the hot fashion photographers, such as Art Kane, Bob Richardson, and David Bailey, the English photographer married to Catherine Deneuve and the inspiration for the Antonioni movie *Blow-Up*. I was totally immersed in the world of fashion. My boss, Albert Koski, was a handsome character who lived and worked in a little house in the Sixteenth Arrondissement where models such as Veruschka, Twiggy, and Marisa Berenson came in and out all day long. My job was simply to open the door, answer the phone, and pretend to all the women who kept calling Albert that he wasn't there. Between the models, the fashion photographers, the ads, and the advertising agencies, however, I began to understand what the fashion world was all about.

Albert represented photographers just as modeling agencies represented models. The idea was to expose the photographers' work through the fashion magazines so that advertisers would hire them. I began to understand the value of image and the flow of the fashion industry. Fabric people make the fabric. Designers make the clothes. Models wear them. Photographers capture them. Magazines show them. Advertisers sell them. Consumers buy them. On and on it

goes, season after season, with new inspirations, new emotions, new faces, and new ways to show it all.

No one in the fashion set acted very serious about work, though most worked very hard. It was important to appear laid-back and cool. Mao Tse-tung's Cultural Revolution in China was purging the country of intellectuals, artists, and freethinkers. What Mao was doing in China was one thing; our perception of it was another. We wore Mao jackets and carried his Little Red Book, but few of us knew what Mao really meant. Through the Beatles and their guru, the Maharaji Mahesh Yogi, we discovered Indian-inspired hippie clothes and smoked pot. In 1968, the smell of marijuana was everywhere.

The streets of Paris were tense. Strikes were closing the airports and the train stations and interrupting mail delivery. Students were occupying the Sorbonne, forcing a call-up of riot police and the first shutdown of the university since the French Revolution. I identified with the rebel students and workers, but in the most superficial way: I was on the barricades between one and two in the morning after leaving Régine's New Jimmy's nightclub, wearing silver bells on my hands and white lipstick. I wasn't one of the stern revolutionaries; I was with the glitzy superficial sympathizers.

I became very close to Marisa Berenson, the successful model who is the great-grandniece of art historian Bernard Berenson and the granddaughter of the famous thirties and forties designer Elsa Schiaparelli. Marisa, who would later appear in the movies *Cabaret* and *Barry Lyndon*, lived in the basement of her grandmother's house near the Champs-Élysées. I have never seen another house like it. Schiaparelli had been influenced by the Surrealist movement and her

friend Jean Cocteau. Her house was rich and grand but witty and eclectic with extravagant objects such as bouquets of feathers and jewels. Her freedom in mixing styles and periods inspired me on how to decorate my own houses later. Marisa and I spent our Saturday afternoons going from movie to movie laughing and sometimes crying. At night we ate langoustines at La Coupole and went dancing at Castel's.

The end of the 1960s was a time of antielitism and democratic creativity, demonstrated by a profusion of costume jewelry. Marisa wore eccentric clothes and had tons of costume jewelry—big belts covered with bold, fake turquoise and coral, rhinestones by the yard, and silver Tibetan chains. In Capri, where I accompanied Marisa to the Fashion Awards, we met the Italian designer Valentino and actor George Hamilton and his future wife, Alana, all of whom were dressed in black with big-buckled belts. We went on to Rome. Cinecittà, the European version of Hollywood, was still going strong and there were lots of film people around town. That meant paparazzi and autograph seekers on the Via Condotti or outside La Taverna Flavia, the exquisite restaurant near the Via Veneto. There were all these magnificent-looking Italian playboys I had met in Cortina, wearing open shirts and gold chains, while we girls wore hairpieces, fake eyelashes, and high platform shoes. It was a lot of fun, but my dream was to go to America.

For all the hedonistic pleasure of being young in Paris, I found Europe oppressive. Students and young people wanted freedom and were risking their lives for it on the streets of Spain and France. In Czechoslovakia, the Prague Spring, which saw liberal reforms under the moderate Communist Party leader Alexander Dubček, was being forced

back into permanent winter by Soviet troops and tanks. The news photos of Czechs fighting back with guns, sticks, and even their bare hands would leave a lasting impression on me.

America was having its own problems in 1968, but to me it seemed more full of hope. Students were exercising their political freedom, pressing for civil rights for minorities and women and protesting the Vietnam War. Though the pictures of war protesters being teargassed and bludgeoned at the Democratic National Convention in Chicago were shocking to us in Europe, the feeling was that America would certainly regain its democratic sense but Czechoslovakia wouldn't. To me, America was the New Frontier, the new world where anything was possible. Nona Gordon, my beautiful red-haired friend from the University of Geneva, was working in Hollywood as assistant to the actor Omar Sharif, and the stories she told me when she visited Geneva and Paris only whetted my appetite more. My dream was to go to Berkeley.

Egon was already in America. Like many young European men of his background, he had gone to New York to enter the training program at Chase Manhattan Bank. We had stayed friends even though he now had an Italian girlfriend. I was surprised by my depth of feeling toward him when he came back to Europe with her for the Christmas holidays and asked me to arrange a dinner party with our mutual friends in Paris. I was so sad the next day, convinced that I'd lost the love of my life, that I went to consult a fortune-teller. Her prophecy, that I would be married and pregnant within six months, made me sadder. I loved Egon, and all I could think of in the metro on my way home was

that he was taking his new girlfriend and not me to his mother's chalet in Cortina for the holidays.

Without a word to anyone, including my boss, I quit my job. I didn't wait for my month's salary. I took Albert's radio, charged a plane ticket to him, and left. I went to Switzerland to visit my father who was there on holiday with my little brother. A week later, Marisa and I went skiing in St. Moritz.

The five-star Badrutt's Palace Hotel in St. Moritz put a high premium on youth and beauty. If you qualified, you got to stay there for practically nothing, though in fairly modest rooms. Marisa and I were in one of those rooms over the Christmas holidays, sometimes heading to the ski slopes and always going to the parties.

Stavros Niarchos, the Greek shipping magnate, gave an annual New Year's Eve party in St. Moritz, and Marisa and I went. Egon's wildly attractive and seductive uncle, Gianni Agnelli, was there, a figure so idolized in Italy that to this day men walk like him, talk like him, and wear their watches over their shirt cuffs as he does. I spent my twenty-first birthday with Marisa fending off the women who were after him, which was not an easy task. Everyone appeared to want to be with someone he or she shouldn't be, including, in my opinion, Egon. And then he came to St. Moritz.

I never did know what happened to his girlfriend, and of course would not ask. All I know is that his room in the Palace was even tinier than ours. More important, he still loved me and invited me to stay with him in New York. My mother gave me an airline ticket for my twenty-first birthday. Three weeks later, I was there. I stayed for two months.

□

DIANE I COULD NOT get enough of New York. I wanted to stay
there, work there, be independent there. New York wasn't
suffocated by class or tradition. New York seemed as young
as I was and infinitely hospitable. I was very happy. Egon
knew everyone, as always. His father, Tassilo, had spent
time in America in the 1930s. A charming Austro-Hungarian
prince, Tassilo had been entertained by rich Texans and
heiresses, such as Marjorie Merriweather Post. When Egon
had come to New York, he was entertained both by friends
of his father, and by the many people he met on his own. He
was, after all, a young, noble, handsome, rich bachelor and a
great catch.

 It was Egon who introduced me to Diana Vreeland,
the reigning queen of fashion at *Vogue*, and to the great design-
ers of the moment, Giorgio di Sant'Angelo and Halston. In
no time at all, I was in the middle of everything and met
everyone. Going at Egon's speed—who in one night could
take in three cocktail parties, one dinner, two balls, and a gay
bar—we covered a lot of ground. In between stops, we fell in
love all over again.

 I didn't want to leave. I kept looking for some way
to support myself in America. I did some modeling at charity
balls, ended up on the cover of some local magazine, and
thought maybe modeling could be my ticket. I went to see
Wilhelmina at her modeling agency. She was a tall, beautiful,
dark-haired ex-model from Germany. She looked carefully at
the pictures Francesco Scavullo had taken of me and politely
turned me down.

 Many of my friends were designers, so fashion was

on my mind, especially after Egon, who loved fashion, would take me shopping and force me to pay attention. All the clothes we saw, however, were either hippie, designer clothes or drip-dry polyester. There was nothing in between, and I sensed an opportunity. I had seen good-looking cotton knit T-shirts in vibrant prints in the south of France. Angelo Ferretti, a flamboyant gambler I had met in Cortina, owned a knitting and printing plant that made T-shirts in Como, Italy. I had the idea to visit him there and see if there was anything I could sell in America.

After two months in New York, I went to Italy at the end of March 1969 and apprenticed myself to Ferretti, learning about spinning, knitting, discharge, and pigment printing. In the midst of my apprenticeship, Egon came to Rome to visit me before setting off on an around-the-world trip. By then we were talking of marriage. He gave me a ring, but I didn't really believe he was serious, nor was I in a terrible hurry to get married. I still wanted to be independent. When Egon left, I went back to work with Ferretti and thought it was Angelo's fast driving between Milan and Florence that was making me nauseous. It wasn't.

I WAS three months pregnant in July 1969, when Egon and I were married in the town hall of Montfort-l'Amaury just outside Paris. My pregnancy barely showed in the Christian Dior wedding dress Marc Bohan designed for me. Five hundred of our friends and relatives came to the reception afterward at the Auberge de la Moutière, a charming provincial inn and restaurant considered the countryside version of Maxim's. The movie *Tom Jones* had recently come out, and I

wanted to replicate the mood and the visuals of the country-side feast. My father hired all the singers and musicians from Rasputin, a Russian nightclub in Paris, to perform at the reception. My father sang and broke a lot of glasses. But there was a shadow over the wedding.

I felt somewhat humiliated about getting married pregnant. I didn't want anyone to think that Egon had had to marry me when the opposite was true. When I had found out I was pregnant, marriage had not been the only option. Abortion was not a major issue in Europe at the time. Many girls I knew in Geneva had had abortions, and I knew the name of the doctor, Dr. S., who had performed them. I had gone to my own doctor in Geneva to find out when I could quietly have an abortion, but my mother told me I was crazy. I was engaged to Egon, she said. I had to let him know I was carrying his child. I couldn't just have an abortion without letting him know.

I still have the telegram in my scrapbook that I sent Egon in Hong Kong: "I am sorry to disturb your journey, but it is impossible to decide alone. Result of the analysis was positive. I am thinking of the Dr. S. solution. I await your decision. Love you more than ever. Diane."

Egon's response was immediate. "No question of S.," his telegram read. "Marriage will occur the 15th of July. Organize it as rapidly as possible. I rejoice. Thinking of you. Love and kisses, Eduard Egon."

The fortune-teller had been right. I would be married and pregnant six months to the day after seeing her in Paris. She hadn't, however, predicted the reaction.

The head of the Fürstenberg family, a cousin of Egon, was outraged that a Fürstenberg could marry a Jewish

girl. The Fürstenbergs are a noble German family, very proud of their blue blood. I was more impressed by the fact that the source of the Danube River was actually in the garden of the Fürstenberg castle near the German-Swiss border town of Donaueschingen. Ironically, when I first visited Donaueschingen a year later, I remember seeing a sign for the town of Ravensbrück on the way to the castle. At the time I didn't know that it was not the same Ravensbrück where my mother had been in prison twenty-five years before, and it knotted my stomach. I quickly dismissed the cloud and smiled at the fact that here I was defying my mother's destiny.

Egon's father, Tassilo, was so pressured by the Fürstenberg patriarch that he would attend our marriage ceremony but ignore the reception.

My mother didn't mind that I was marrying a German. She liked Egon very much. Egon's Italian mother, Clara, didn't seem disturbed, either. My mother and I had met with Clara at her home outside Venice to plan the invitations. With only six weeks to organize the wedding, everything was in such a rush that there was no way to know if Clara's enthusiasm was genuine. But I had moments of uneasiness. I remember taking a walk in Clara's garden alone, talking to the child I was carrying, and saying out loud that I was going to be successful to prove myself to this disapproving family. I had that fire in me both for me and for the baby inside me. Together we would show the world.

I went back to work at Ferretti's factory in the midst of the wedding preparations. "I'm pregnant, I'm getting married, and I'm going back to America," I told them. "So let's put a collection together." Egon was very enthusiastic. From

the beginning, he had encouraged me to work, to have a career, to continue what I was doing with Ferretti because it was important. I never doubted Egon or our love. I was starting my adult life where most fairy tales end, by marrying the prince.

Many European newspapers covered our wedding, as did *Women's Wear Daily* and *Vogue*. "A gypsy brilliance—young, joyful, high-key—lighted the French provincial wedding of Diane Halfin and Prince Eduard Egon von und zu Fürstenberg," the *Vogue* story began. After a short honeymoon sailing the fjords of Norway, Egon and I went to a little house on Sardinia's Costa Smeralda that his mother had bought us as a wedding present.

We filled the house with close friends, such as Nona, Marisa, the actor Hiram Keller. I remember one night on the terrace, J. Paul Getty Jr. reciting poetry while his beautiful young wife, Talitha, was dancing under the stars. They were the golden couple of the sixties, it seemed that the world belonged to them. Then she died tragically of a drug overdose about two years later. We all wore tiny bikinis and embroidered caftans, swam in the turquoise water, gave parties, and, for two months, lived *la dolce vita* in the sun. In between swimming and sunbathing, Marisa and I ironed our hair on the ironing board to achieve the fashion demand of long, straight hair. It would be years before I would come to terms with my curly hair.

In the fall, Egon flew back to New York and I followed by ship. Since I was really moving to America and no longer just going for a visit, I wanted to arrive slowly. I wanted to come into New York Harbor past the Statue of Liberty just as every immigrant with a dream for the future.

I went to Ferretti's factory, picked up the dress samples I had had made, and put them into a trunk. In September 1969, I sailed for New York aboard the Italian liner, *Raffaello.* I was twenty-two.

HOW NOT
TO START
A BUSINESS

N̲o̲ ̲o̲n̲e̲ took me seriously at first, and I can't blame them. There I was in Ronnie Ruskin's top-floor office at Best & Co., and the president of the prestigious Fifth Avenue store was looking at a very pregnant girl stuffed into a Pucci dress and showing him little jersey dresses out of a big Vuitton suitcase. I can't remember whether he liked the dresses. What I remember is going back downstairs and bursting into tears on the street.

It was rush hour, I couldn't get a taxi, and the suitcase felt as heavy as a steamer trunk. All I could think of was Mia Farrow in *Rosemary's Baby* when she struggled to escape, pregnant, with her suitcase. The next day I made my retail rounds in a limousine, but the struggle at Best became a metaphor for my first two years in the fashion business.

I had no idea what I was doing. Being so young, however, I would turn ignorance to advantage. Two months after I had my son, Alexandre, in January 1970, I got an appointment with Diana Vreeland, the editor of *Vogue*. That I dared to show the reigning arbiter of fashion and taste my little dresses seems cheeky to me now, but she had consented to see me. As much as I was an inexperienced young girl, I was also a European princess and embraced socially by the

city. The combination opened doors, even Vreeland's—if you dared knock.

 I was, of course, terrified of Mrs. Vreeland. When I'd been with Egon during my first stay in New York and had thought that maybe I could model to support myself, I had gone to see her. "Chin up—up—UP!" she commanded me before it became clear that modeling was not my path to the future. Returning to *Vogue* less than a year later, with my suitcase and my samples of twelve or so dresses in three styles, was even more intimidating.

Red. I'd never seen such bright red as the lacquered walls of her office. But everything about Diana Vreeland was expansive. There were racks of clothes in her office, tables full of jewelry, pictures everywhere. On her desk was a lit Rigaud candle and its zebra box was a pencil holder. I waited nervously for her to appear, surrounded by several of her editors and assistants, all dressed in black. Her loud, distinctive laughter preceded her as she came down the hall.

"Chin up—UP!" she greeted me in her customary commanding style. She, too, was dressed in black with a huge Kenneth Jay Lane brooch on her shoulder, her omnipresent cigarette holder in her mouth, and her nails as red as her office walls. I showed her samples of the rumpled shirtdress, the T-shirt dress, and the skirt with a wrap top and watched anxiously as she tried a few pieces on two pencil-thin girls who would become stars—the dark-haired, exotic Pat Cleveland as a model and the red-haired, cat-eyed Loulou de La Falaise as the muse for Yves Saint Laurent. "Terrific, terrific, terrific," she said to my amazement in her theatrical voice. "How clever of you." The *r*'s were still rolling as I found

ABOVE: My father's mother, Sarah Halfin. I never met her, but my father worshipped her. When my father decided not to go back to Russia after attending school in Belgium, she wrote him a letter that said, "May your refugee condition bring you good luck." It did.

ABOVE RIGHT: My mother's father, Moshe Nahmias. I remember him well. He was handsome and very calm. He loved birds and flowers. I would visit him and read him my little books.

RIGHT: With my parents, Lily and Leon Halfin, in Brussels.

Unless otherwise noted, all photos courtesy of the author.

My brother, Philippe, was born on December 13, 1952, a week after St. Nicolas, the Belgian Father Christmas. That year, instead of asking for a present, I had written to him to ask for a little brother. St. Nicolas did bring me a little brother, though he arrived a week late.

My first year in school, my kindergarten year. My mother had attended the same school and we had had the same headmistress, Mlle. Gilette (standing behind me). This is probably why I was chosen to blow out the candles on the school's seventy-fifth-anniversary cake. This photo appeared on the front page of *Le Soir*, the leading Belgian newspaper. My first try at being a "cover girl."

Me alone. Not a picture that I like, and certainly a picture that I disliked at the time, but you can clearly see my curly hair.

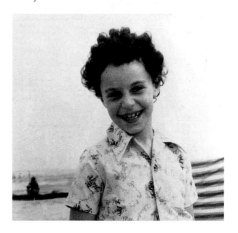

ABOVE LEFT: My father and I. I loved my father and he loved me. He was extremely affectionate, a trait I inherited from him and passed on to my own children.

BELOW LEFT: This is my favorite photograph of my father. As I get older, it seems as though I look more and more like him. I see his face each time I look in the mirror.

BELOW RIGHT: My mother in front of her apartment in Geneva, Switzerland. Looking back, I now realize that I inherited all my curiosity and passion for life from her.

My Stroud Court class photo with our teachers and our headmaster, Mr. Underwood. That's me in the back row, fourth from the right.

Myself, Deanna, and Helena at Stroud Court. Deanna was French and Helena, whose father was a soccer player, was from Iceland. Deanna and I went on to study Spanish at the University of Madrid.

OPPOSITE:

TOP LEFT: Philippe and I in Spain on vacation with our mother. I remember the silk print dress I was wearing: I had bought it with my own money in Oxford.

TOP RIGHT: My first boyfriend, Sohrab. He was a handsome Persian boy, studying architecture at Oxford.

BOTTOM: Me at age 20 at the swimming pool of the Intercontinental Hotel in Geneva, where I was studying Economics at the University of Geneva and working part time at IOS, the fund-of-funds company founded by Bernie Kornfeld. (Donald Stampfli)

Egon and I arriving at a nightclub in Rome on the night we got engaged in May 1969. The next day he went on a trip around the world. He came back two weeks before the wedding. *(Reg Gray/WWD)*

ABOVE RIGHT: The *Town & Country* cover couple. Very 70s look: a hair piece, false eyelashes, and a huge necklace designed by David Webb; unlike my handsome husband who looks good in a simple black turtleneck. (Town & Country, *photo by Francesco Scavullo*)

RIGHT BELOW: Alexandre, Egon, myself, and Tatiana in our Park Avenue apartment in 1971. The ages of all four of us totaled fifty years. (Town & Country)

The rain of rice for good luck. The day of my wedding, July 16, 1969, was a beautiful, hot day in Montfort l'Amaury, outside Paris. Behind us is Angelo Ferretti, my friend who owned the factory that would later manufacture "the dress." *(Berry Berenson Perkins)*

Draping on a dress form. My friend Mary Russel, the American photographer "à la mode" in Paris, took this picture of me as part of a reportage to illustrate the modern woman (I was pregnant with Alexandre at the time). *(Mary Russel)*

Diana Vreeland, the grande dame of fashion. This extraordinary woman helped and inspired everyone in the industry for decades. She loved young, talented people and was fantastically supportive of them. *(Horst)*

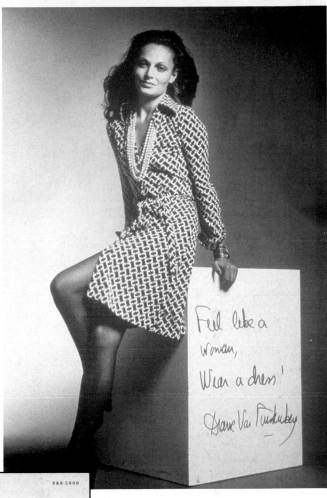

Feel like a
woman,
Wear a dress!

Diane Von Furstenberg

Me and my first favorite dress, the shirtdress, in a navy and white geometric print, with three strings of pearls, a Bulgari snake watch, and high heels . . . sitting on a white cube. My French friend Roger Prigent took the picture. On it I wrote, "Feel like a woman, wear a dress!" and signed my name underneath. The signature was born. (*Roger Prigent*)

I was so encouraged when I received this letter from Diana Vreeland that I had it framed. (*Courtesy of the Estate of Diana Vreeland*)

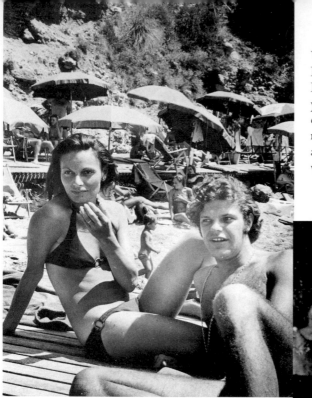

With Egon on the beach in Ischia in the summer of 1972. I love this picture. We were so young and beautiful! Our children and both of our mothers were there as well, and during the week I would work at Ferretti's factory.

Egon and I in Dallas, 1972, at the Crystal Ball, given by Mary Wells and designed by Cecil Beaton. I thought everyone was very old, and I didn't have a good time, but this picture (which would run in *Newsweek* magazine) changed my life. *(Larry Reese*/Dallas News)

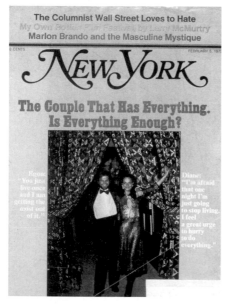

The Columnist Wall Street Loves to Hate

My Own Route. A Girl Feature, by Larry McMurtry

Marlon Brando and the Masculine Mystique

8 CENTS FEBRUARY 5, 1973

NEW YORK

The Couple That Has Everything. Is Everything Enough?

Upon seeing the above photo, *New York* magazine's founder and editor in chief Clay Felker, commissioned Linda Bird Francke to write a story on "this hot, young New York couple." That article would bring about the beginning of the end of our marriage. (New York)

In Ponza, Italy, with Italian journalist Jas Gawronski. Jas was ten years older than me, and he was serious and kind. He healed the wounds of my broken marriage.

The beginning of an era: Bianca Jagger's birthday party at Halston's townhouse with Bob Colacello, Halston, Barry Diller, Barbara Allen, and myself. After dinner, we were all taken to a new club that had just opened: Studio 54.

Andy Warhol, with my great friend, producer Franco Rossellini (the funniest Italian in town), and writer Bob Colacello.

Being interviewed by Bill Boggs with fellow designers Georgio di Sant'Angelo, Bill Blass, and Perry Ellis. *(Jim Lorelli)*

After lunch at La Grenouille, the best French restaurant in New York at the time, with Pierre Bergé, Yves Saint Laurent's partner; Yves (looking handsome); myself; Bianca Jagger; and Marina Schiano. *(Peter Zachary Simin, WWD)*

With Italian designer Valentino, a great friend who makes the most beautiful ball gowns and is the most gracious host when you visit him in his villas all over the world. *(Nick Machalaba, WWD)*

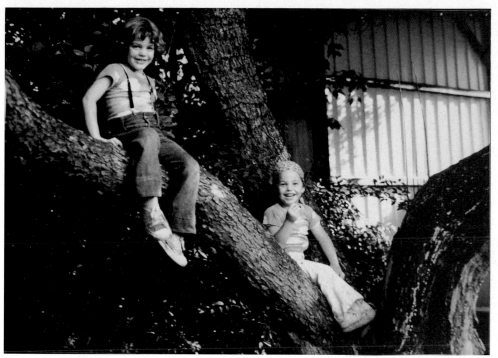

Alexandre and Tatiana climbing an apple tree during their
first summer at Cloudwalk.

One of Barry's first visits to Cloudwalk and his first introduction to the
children. *(Burt Glinn, Magnum Photos)*

At a personal appearance at Rich's department store in Atlanta. The store had these mannequins made to look like "me"—long before cloning!

Twenty-nine years old and on the front page of *The Wall Street Journal*. Things are looking good. (The Wall Street Journal)

Once Upon a Time, A Princess Made It With the Hoi Polloi

Diane von Furstenberg Reigns Over Fashion Empire Now; The Ubiquitous Print Dress

By KAREN SCHNEIDER

March 22, 1976. There I am on the cover of *Newsweek*. Barry, always thoughtful, commissioned a photographer to take pictures of newsstands in all different neighborhoods and put them in an album.

With California governor
Jerry Brown, just after he
announced his candidacy for
president in 1976. I gave him a
party to introduce him to
New York.

My first visit to the White
House with President Gerald
Ford, escorted by Luis
Estevez, the California
designer who dressed the
First Lady. (*Official White House
photo*)

myself in the corridor, folding the dresses back into the suitcase.

It was one of Diana Vreeland's fashion editors, the dark, long-haired, beautiful assistant, Kezia Keeble Hovey, who gave me twenty minutes that would shape my life. Fashion Week is coming up in New York, she told me. List your name in the Fashion Calendar. Take a suite for a week at the Gotham Hotel on Fifth Avenue at Fifty-fifth Street, where the California fashion houses will be showing. I didn't know where the Gotham Hotel was or what the Fashion Calendar was, but I knew I wanted to be on it. "Can I use your phone?" I asked her. When I got back to our apartment that night, the reality began to set in that I was starting a business.

Kenneth Jay Lane, the costume jewelry designer and friend of Egon's, sent me to his lawyer, Gerald Mandelbaum, who looked at me with amusement when I told him I wanted to set up a company. "And how do you want the company name to read?" he asked with a smile.

"Diane Furstenberg," I replied.

"Oh, do *'Von Furstenberg,'*" he said. "It sounds much better."

I MADE MY first sale at the Gotham Hotel in April 1970 to Sarah Fredericks, a little shop in New Jersey. The order was very small, but it was a beginning. I had only the twelve or so cotton knit dress samples in a few prints and a limited collection of assorted printed silk knit tent dresses Ferretti had made up for me out of leftover fabric. To show them, I had one model, Jane Forth, who was one of Andy Warhol's

girls from the Factory, as his studio was known; a startlingly pale-skinned, minuscule eighteen-year-old with totally plucked eyebrows.

I organized a small fashion show in the banquet room of the hotel to introduce the dresses and invited all of Egon's friends and contacts. I didn't have the money to hire professional models, so I called a modeling school out of the Yellow Pages and got twelve students. It was scarcely a fashion show, but I didn't know any better. So I improvised. Someone had given me a bunch of tulips, and I gave each girl a tulip to carry for the finale.

I had no idea who the buyers were who came in and out of the suite all week long, but I was attentive to all of them, even when they were rude. One woman, Rose Wuhl, who turned out to be an important fashion guru, walked in, looked at the cotton dresses and announced, "They're junk, but they'll sell." Before I knew it, five people from Bloomingdale's appeared to place orders.

Other buyers passed on the dresses altogether. I remember Charlott Kramer, the famous dress buyer from Saks, looking quickly at the dresses and leaving without a word. The rejection, however, would be temporary. Eighteen months later Charlott would see the exact same dresses, and this time buy them. She would become our absolutely best account, my most fervent customer, and my loyal friend.

The fine silk knit tent dresses turned out to be a surprising success. Fred and Gale Hayman, the pioneers of Rodeo Drive in Los Angeles, and the owners of Giorgio Beverly Hills, bought the entire assortment for their California boutique. The order for sixty or so dresses seemed huge to me at the time, especially when I had to pack and ship

them myself, and would prove invaluable. The tent dresses would soon appear at Hollywood parties on Ali McGraw, Candice Bergen, and Rita Hayworth and be a great help in establishing my name on the West Coast.

Help on the East Coast came from Egon's friends. Kenny Lane urged fashion editors to come see me during Fashion Week. Bill Blass made some calls for me, mainly to the press. Obviously, he didn't think of me as a competitor. Nobody thought of me as a competitor. There were a lot of Europeans coming to New York trying to sell things, so it wasn't so odd. And besides, we were all friends.

Egon and I were known as a "fun couple," a young, attractive European girl married to a young, attractive European aristocrat. We entertained often, and our apartment became a sort of salon for young people like ourselves who were trying to make their way in America. Whether they were in corporate training programs like Egon or making or selling things, we were all chasing the American dream.

Elsa Peretti and Marina Schiano, two tall, extroverted Italian girls who emerged on the seventies scene as models and favorites of Diana Vreeland because, in some ways, she thought they both looked like her, were close friends. Later Elsa would become a sculptor and a successful jewelry designer for Tiffany, and Marina would work with Saint Laurent and would later become a photographer and a stylist. Jewelry designer Paloma Picasso, the daughter of the master, was around, as was the writer Fran Lebowitz, who was driving a taxicab at the time and incubating her book *Metropolitan Life.*

A lot of them were members of Halston's court. Halston represented American chic and was very much at the

center of things in the early 1970s. He was designing Ultrasuede dresses and tie-dyed caftans for Babe Paley and had a shop and atelier on Madison Avenue. He was a good bit older and more established, but he loved to surround himself with younger, talented people.

Joe Eula, the artist and illustrator, was his friend and ours, as was Loulou de La Falaise. Joel Schumacher, who was doing the windows at Henri Bendel and would go on to become a screenwriter and later a major movie director in Hollywood, was part of the group, as was Berry Berenson, the photographer and Marisa's sister, who would later marry the actor Anthony Perkins. Giorgio di Sant'Angelo, a truly original designer who used a lot of jersey and stretch fabrics in his clothes and was a great inspiration to me, was also a frequent guest, as was Kenny Lane, who would later rent one of the cottages at Cloudwalk from me. We were of different ages and different backgrounds, but we shared the same attitudes.

Andy Warhol also became a friend of sorts. I met him through Jane Forth, my first house model at the Gotham Hotel. Andy was a silent presence, a voyeur who always had a tape recorder or a camera in his hand to record rather than participate. "Oh gee, that's great," he'd say in his distinctive little voice about everything and everyone.

He became a fixture at our parties and at every party we went to; with the five or six courtiers he always brought with him. There was Fred Hughes, the Houston dandy; Bob Colacello, the Georgetown graduate who became the editor of *Interview;* the handsome twins Jed and Jay Johnson; Paul Morrissey, the director of his movies; and others. Andy was a major influence and catalyst in New York life. I don't think I

ever had a long or serious conversation with Andy, but we acknowledged each other and shared an interest in antique jewelry. We were both amongst the first clients of Fred Leighton, who now has the biggest collection of antique jewelry in the world at his store on Madison Avenue but who then dealt in jewelry out of the back of his shop in Greenwich Village, where he sold Mexican dresses.

Egon liked to collect modern art, and one night Andy asked if he could take Polaroid photos of me for a silk-screen portrait. The only white wall I could find in our apartment was in the kitchen. To lend a little cachet to the setting, I held my arm over my head, which made the shots look quite odd. It would be months before I dared look at the finished portraits. I didn't think two Polaroids taken at night in the kitchen looking somewhat like a deodorant ad would be in any way flattering or glamorous. But I liked the portrait well enough. Andy gave me one, and I bought three, two of them now hang over my office desk.

I would pose for Andy again in 1983 or '84 for a series called *Beauties.* He made me and everyone else in that series put white makeup on our faces. When he died in 1987, I bought everything he'd done of me from his estate, except for one of the early ones, which now hangs in the Warhol Museum in Pittsburgh.

Egon and I went out a lot in the early 1970s. A lot. We went to openings, closings, previews, balls, benefits, and private parties and became staples in the society columns. Because of our visibility, Valentino, Halston, and Yves Saint Laurent gave me their clothes to wear. I had fun dressing up, I had many ballgowns, which I wore out at night, along with

lots of makeup and bracelets to the elbow on both arms. It was interesting to enter the fashion world through two different doors: as a client and as a designer.

During the height of the winter season in New York, we averaged four invitations a night, mostly from people we'd never met. I remember having dinner with Salvador Dalí and his wife, the dark and petite Gala, at the St. Regis Hotel and with the Duke and Duchess of Windsor at the Waldorf Towers. The duke and duchess were very elegant and perfectly pleasant but did not impress me very much. Dalí, on the other hand, fascinated me, and so did his wife and muse, Gala, who had previously been married to the great French poet Paul Éluard.

We also traveled a lot. In between my trips to Ferretti's factory in Italy, we circulated between our house in Sardinia, Egon's mother's chalet in Cortina, and a rented house in the Pines on Fire Island next to Halston's. For one entire July, we listened to Elsa Peretti and Marina Schiano fight in Italian while Joe Eula designed scarves with Loulou de La Falaise. The great film director Luchino Visconti, who had recently made *Death in Venice*, with my friend Marisa, also spent a few days at our house there. I remember walking the beach together at sunset, going through the dunes, and ending with tea on the terrace of a house at Cherry Grove, pretentiously called Belvedere. It was very funny to be sitting there, watching the amused and disgusted expression on the face of one of the greatest esthetes of all time.

Our jet-setting lifestyle made good copy for the social columnists. *Women's Wear Daily*, *The New York Times*, and the New York *Post* ran articles about me and my first collection

during Fashion Week in 1970, though the emphasis was more on me than on the dresses. Eugenia Shepherd in her New York *Post* column "Inside Fashion" concentrated the first two paragraphs on the parties the "Prince and Princess Egon von Fürstenberg" were invited to and didn't mention my clothes until the third paragraph. Though the dresses were essential to me, to the press the little dresses I was selling were an afterthought.

Everybody was intrigued by this young princess who was making simple go-everywhere dresses instead of ball gowns for the elite. And it justified their stories. "In Private Life, Diane is known as Princess Egon von Fürstenberg," ran the headline on the article in *Women's Wear Daily* that pronounced me "New York's newest designer." Bernadine Morris at *The New York Times* titled her story "For the Princess, a Stylish Business."

Those first three articles were invaluable in launching my new business and added another important account to my first sales. Across the street from the Gotham Hotel was the Revlon beauty salon, where I went one day during Fashion Week to have my hair done. "Are you Diane Von Furstenberg?" asked a small blond woman under the hair dryer next to mine. When I told her yes, she introduced herself. "My name is Phyllis Davidson, and I'm a Lord & Taylor buyer," she said. "I want to come see you." She did and placed what seemed like a large order at the time for cotton T-shirt dresses and shirtdresses in a chain print. I remember the specific print well because it would be on a personal appearance for the launch of these dresses with Phyllis at the Lord & Taylor in Hartford that I would discover Connecti-

cut for the first time. It was October, and the colors of the fall foliage were so extraordinary that I decided that Connecticut was where I would like to have a home.

The first publicity certainly helped to get orders from the stores for two hundred or so dresses. Perhaps some of the naïveté and spontaneity of my first fashion show was attractive to the fashion editors. Filling the orders, however, was a nightmare, especially after the demand grew when Diana Vreeland ran one of the dresses in *Vogue* soon after I'd seen her in the spring of 1970.

I had no office, no staff. I stored the dresses in the dining room of our apartment and processed the orders with office supplies I bought at Woolworth. Because the orders were relatively small, I had to fly to Italy once a month to beg Ferretti to fill them. His printing, knitting, and sewing factories were designed to make T-shirts in mass production. He couldn't stop his machines to cut such small quantities, let alone make special prints. I had to beg, cry, and use every ounce of charm. "Stick with me," I pleaded. "I promise you will be rewarded." Finally he would do the clothes as a personal favor and a sign of faith rather than as a professional investment.

The shipments from Italy were often late and sometimes wrong, leaving me in some disfavor with store buyers who had ordered them. They did not complain, though, because the clothes sold quickly anyway. I spent what seemed like years in the customs warehouses at Kennedy Airport breaking down the bulk shipments for reshipment to individual stores. The first shipment, in the winter of 1970, was the worst. The fabric content of each item was written in Italian, and for hours I sat in tears on the floor in the freezing cold

warehouse of Air India in front of the open boxes, crossing out all the labels in Italian and rewriting them in English. I couldn't have been farther from the glamorous princess life being written about in the newspapers.

I was also pregnant again, just three months after giving birth to Alexandre. He had been delivered by emergency cesarean section on January 25, 1970, after I had been in labor for sixteen hours. Tatiana was due in February 1971, and the doctor advised me to have another cesarean, this one planned, because I had hardly healed from the last. He gave me a two-week window, and I chose February 16. Two and five added up to seven as did one and six, which I took to be a good omen. And it was. Tatiana was as healthy and beautiful as her brother, making me a very happy and proud mother of two at the age of twenty-four. I was so young, I hadn't even had the time to wish for children before they were already there. I had not thought I would be very maternal and yet their births changed my life. They became my center, gave new sense to my existence, and forced me to be aware and responsible forever.

I was back in the warehouse a week after Tatiana was born to sort and ship the spring orders. We had a nanny to help look after the children when they were very young. To house everyone comfortably, including my mother, who spent eight months a year with us, we bought the apartment adjoining ours in our building on Park Avenue and broke through the wall. I spent every minute I could with the children, whom I loved with a passion more powerful than anything I had ever felt before. I also loved my work and realized how important it was going to be for me and them.

I felt a tremendous urgency. I was afraid that one night

I was just going to stop living and never have time to tell my small children everything I had to tell them. I was also worried that I wouldn't have the time to achieve the independence that was still considered a luxury for many women in the 1970s, but was increasingly important to my identity.

Though Egon was perfectly able and willing to support me, I wanted very much to be financially independent. Nothing makes me more miserable than to have to ask for money. At one point, when I couldn't cover my invoices at Ferretti's factory, I pawned a diamond ring that Egon and my father had given me when Tatiana was born. I was able to buy the ring back two weeks later, paying huge interest, but it meant that much to me to go about my business without any outside help.

I had no focus groups, no marketing surveys, no plan. All I had was an instinct that women wanted a fashion option besides hippie clothes, bell-bottoms, and stiff pant-suits that hid their femininity. Though the unisex look was hot in the seventies, I was sure there was a need for simple little sexy dresses that made women feel like women. And the dresses made sense. They were sexy and practical, washable and wrinkle proof. The prints were colorful and lighthearted, the fabric soft and supple.

The fabric was the most important. When women tried on the dresses, it was the feel of the cotton-and-rayon blend that really sold them. So did the look. What made the dresses special was that they looked like nothing on hangers but were so flattering on. You wore the clothes, the clothes didn't wear you—which was rare at the time.

□

THE DEMOCRATIZATION of fashion was just beginning in the 1970s. The very privileged could go to the fashion shows in Paris twice a year to see and buy very expensive made-to-order designer clothes at the couture houses such as Dior, Saint Laurent, Balmain, Givenchy, and Lanvin. Dressmakers from all over Europe would also attend the fashion shows, as would selected journalists. The most influential by far were John Fairchild, the chairman of *Women's Wear Daily*, and Diana Vreeland at *Vogue*, who between the two of them determined what styles, colors, and hemlines America—and the world— would wear that season. Everyone lived by their pronouncements. The dressmakers would buy one or two patterns at the collections that they then reproduced for their customers in their various cities in the designer fabric they had bought from the fabric manufacturers. That brought the price down somewhat in Europe, but the real deal was in America.

Buyers for two inexpensive American stores, Ohrbach's and Alexander's, also came to the fashion shows in Paris. They too would buy some of the designer patterns, but they would then have them executed by some Seventh Avenue manufacturer and sell them very cheaply. It was the hot thing in Europe to come to New York when these clothes were available. There was a lot of excitement on the third floor of Ohrbach's when the limited number of early copies made in the original fabrics would appear. It was thrilling to buy an authentic Saint Laurent dress for only $150, and Egon and I shopped there all the time.

The true revolution in fashion began when avant-garde Saint Laurent became the first designer to present his own line of *prêt-à-porter*, or ready-to-wear, clothes. His line and the boutique he created to sell them in on the Left Bank

in Paris were called Saint Laurent Rive Gauche and were the beginning of designer ready-to-wear in Europe.

Designers such as Kenzo, the Paris-based Japanese designer, and the French designer André Courrèges also offered their own ready-to-wear lines. Kenzo's clothes were colorful with ethnic inspirations, while Courrèges's tended to be stiff and tailored. If you put his signature pastel, white-rimmed A-line dresses on the floor, they would stand by themselves. Personally, I still loved to wear the hippie clothes designed by the English designer Ossie Clark and by Jean Bouquin, the sexy French designer of nightclub clothes and friend of Brigitte Bardot, with their poetic look of big, ruffled shirts, crushed-velvet pants, and big clunky jewelry. But the hippie "make love, not war" look was not easy to translate into daily life for women who went to work and had children.

Though I didn't realize it at the time, perhaps the little dresses I was designing were a bridge between the radical side of me, which wore the shortest, tiniest hot pants, a printed Saint Laurent Rive Gauche blazer, and the highest platform shoes at night, and the more conservative side, which wore little dresses during the day. My life, after all, was quite proper. I was living on Park Avenue. I had a husband who went to Wall Street every morning wearing a suit and tie, two small children, and a nanny, and in the evening I went out to cocktail parties. Though I may have been more bohemian in my heart, I related to the other mothers I saw every day picking up their children at nursery school and play groups. No one was making a proper little dress for them. So I would.

I was up to thirty accounts by 1972, just two years after I had shown my first collection. I was still doing every-

thing myself: designing the prints, showing the clothes, taking the orders, handling the invoices, sorting out the shipments in the warehouse at JFK, and packing and re-shipping the clothes.

I was in Brazil for carnival when I came to the conclusion that I couldn't go on working in this amateurish way. Either I had to get serious or stop. Egon and I had just been photographed by the famous photographer Francesco Scavullo for the cover of *Town & Country*, but the emphasis on me was still as part of a social couple and not as a designer. I didn't like that. When I returned to New York, I decided to get more serious about my work, to make a real business out of it.

The next natural step was to become a division of some large Seventh Avenue company. That way the company could handle the distribution and the business details while I could concentrate on the designing and making of the clothes. But of the three companies I went to, none, it turned out, shared my vision.

The president of Jonathan Logan looked at the samples I was still lugging around in a suitcase and put me in touch with the manager of one of his divisions. "These are little boutiquey clothes. This is not volume," the manager scoffed, showing me the horrible polyester dresses they made. I got a similar brush-off at David Crystal, another Seventh Avenue company.

Only Johnny Pomerantz, the son of the owner of Leslie Fay, a large, successful Seventh Avenue company, showed interest. Perhaps it was because he was a young man and I was a young woman in my unbuttoned little shirtdress showing off my legs. Or perhaps it was because I had a copy

of Larry Collins and Dominique La Pierre's *O Jerusalem!* with me, which, for some reason, surprised him. But it was Johnny who proved my mother's credo that what seemed like the worst thing to happen to you could be the best. No, he said, the dresses were not for his company. But yes, he would help me.

In what proved to be the most significant advice I would ever receive, Johnny Pomerantz urged me to go into business for myself. "I think you do have a good product, even though it's not for us," he told me. "But you don't need us. You don't need anybody. Take a showroom on Seventh Avenue, hire a salesman, and just do it."

I panicked. I was twenty-five years old in a strange country with no experience whatsoever. A showroom meant signing a lease. Seventh Avenue could mean dealing with the unions. Though you don't in fact deal with the unions when you import, I had heard stories about them. "How do I do that?" I asked Johnny. "I don't know any salesmen."

"I do," he said.

Within days I was negotiating with Dick Conrad, a thirty-nine-year-old entrepreneur who was looking for a new business to run. I had very little money to offer him, but he was willing to gamble. "Give me three hundred dollars a week and twenty-five percent of the company, and I'll do it with you," he said.

In April 1972, I reorganized my company. My partnership with Dick Conrad started with only $1,000, with $250 coming from Dick. But we were officially in business.

We took a showroom at 530 Seventh Avenue, and I painted the walls brown, bought tables and desks from the Door Store, and hung Andy Warhol flower posters on the

walls. Ferretti helped out by giving me a long line of credit. I would pay him in ninety-day cycles, while I would get paid in sixty days. So that Dick would understand what he was selling, I had a few shirts made for him out of Ferretti's fabric.

The first months were a scramble, but we got through them. The volume of orders grew by the week, and by the end of 1972, the business had grown to wholesale revenues totaling $1.2 million. A year later, the business had multiplied sevenfold. And all because of one little dress: the Wrap.

PROBABLY until I die, women will tell me, "Oh, when I got married" or "When I got divorced" or "When I fell in love" or "When I got promoted I wore one of your wrap dresses." For some reason, this dress would become an icon for many women in the 1970s and a cultural phenomenon. Suburban housewives and New York lawyers bought and wore the wrap. So did actresses such as Candice Bergen, Cybill Shepherd, and Mary Tyler Moore; political wives such as Betty Ford; activists such as Angela Davis; feminists such as Gloria Steinem; models such as Cheryl Tiegs. The wrap dress transcended generations, geographical distinctions, social and economic differences. I couldn't believe it.

The idea for the wrap dress had not come out of a strategy session or a market analysis. I had gotten the idea by watching Julie Nixon Eisenhower on television wearing a wrap top and skirt of mine she had ordered from the Lord & Taylor catalog. Why not combine the two pieces into one? I thought.

Ferretti, as usual, was difficult. Though the volume

of orders was multiplying by the week, he complained that the orders weren't enough to justify reconfiguring his machines. On the one hand, he was very supportive, but on the other, he pressured me to increase the orders. When I asked him to add the new wrap style, once again I had to beg, cajole, promise, and plead with him as well as with his factory workers, who had to put in extra time. I brought them press clips and articles to make them feel proud of the product they were working on and ate countless pasta lunches with them in the factories. Thank God I spoke Italian and could therefore talk directly to the supervisors, the ironers, the pattern makers, the sewers—everyone in the factory. By establishing a dialogue and a personal relationship with the workers, I became part of the factory. As a result, everyone did more for me.

The first wrap dress arrived in 1973 in a wood-grain print. The dress was nothing, really—just a few yards of fabric with two sleeves and a wide wrap sash. But the V-neck wrap design fit a woman's body like no other dress: snug around the chest and arms, tied flatteringly slim around the waist, full enough over the legs for a woman to take an unrestricted stride, yet tight enough to show off her bottom. Dressed up with jewelry and high heels, the dress was ready to wear to a serious lunch or dinner; dressed down with a camisole and a lower heel, it was comfortable to wear in an office. But mostly, the wrap was sexy in the way many women wanted to feel: chic, practical, and seductive.

In the years since, all sorts of social significance has been read into the dress. To some, the wrap became a manifesto for the liberated woman of the 1970s. The dress fit in with the woman's revolution by allowing the millions of

women going off to work to be well dressed and out the door in a minute without worrying about wrinkles, buttons, zippers, hooks and eyes. The wrap also fit in with the sexual revolution; a woman who chose to could be out of it in less than a minute.

The dress spread across a wide spectrum in the 1970s and represented many things to many different women. The wrap was featured in *The Official Preppy Handbook* and in Richard Reeves's 1977 book, *Convention,* about the 1976 Democratic National Convention. It will probably be on my tombstone: "Here Lies the Woman Who Designed the Wrap Dress."

I was flattered that the wrap generated such attention, though I preferred the shirtdress and rarely wore the wrap myself. I had no idea that one day it would hang in the Smithsonian Institution. I just thought it was a good dress.

In 1972, I ran my first ad in *Women's Wear Daily* to announce the opening of our showroom. I didn't have an advertising agency, a model, or a fancy photographer. I asked a friend of mine to take a picture of me sitting on a white cube, wearing one of my printed shirtdresses. Looking at the photograph, I picked up a pen and wrote on the cube in my own handwriting: *"Feel like a woman, wear a dress! Diane Von Furstenberg."* That handwritten copy line and my signature in the first ad I created would appear on every dress tag for the next decade and become my registered trademark. I had inadvertently turned my signature into a brand.

Bloomingdale's followed my ad with its own ad for my dresses, but there was a last-minute mix-up with the model and the buyer said, "Well, let's just use Diane." I didn't know if any other designers had ever appeared in their

own ads, but it seemed a natural solution at the time. From that moment on, however, the stores would identify me and the product so closely that they would insist on featuring me in every ad, whether an illustration or a photograph. The result would be a total identity of me, the product, and the brand.

I have always understood this symbiosis and agreed with it, but the execution was really difficult. The hardest part of my work has always been to be photographed, to be totally out in front. Even now stores insist on using my image, which is hard for me when I think I look terrible. But the truth is that even when I posed for ads twenty-five years ago, I thought I looked bad.

The American press was building my self-image somewhat, though the descriptions of me made me laugh. One newspaper described me as an "exotic beauty," which I found rather exciting. In the cover story *Town & Country* ran of Egon and me in March 1972, Egon was described as "blond, tall, with cherubic boyish features" and I was depicted as "dark, small, with the sultriness of a biblical temptress." I don't know how insecure biblical temptresses were, but I was still spending an inordinate amount of time and money having my hair blown and straightened.

Strangely, what I found rewarding was going on the road to make personal appearances. The department stores made great use of my title—"The Princess Von Furstenberg is holding court in our NY Sutton Place department tomorrow" ran one early Bloomingdale's ad—and there is no question that the title added glitz to the appearances. Everybody wanted to invite me to their stores. More important to me

was that I was meeting the women who were buying my clothes and getting to know America.

Between 1973 and 1976, I traveled constantly to promote the clothes at department stores. The dresses were very light, so everything went into such a tiny little bag that I didn't have to check it. To pass the time on the planes, I stared at the map of the United States and memorized the states. I can still list alphabetically every state and every state capital in the country. On one tour, I did fourteen cities in thirteen days.

The children were used to seeing me coming and going, and though we spent every weekend together, I missed them terribly. I often took very early flights from New York instead of traveling more leisurely the night before so I could spend the evening with the children. As often as I could, I tried to fly back to New York in time for their supper. But the lessons I was learning on my travels were invaluable.

THE AMERICAN RETAIL WORLD was very different from that of Europe. In Europe we had only boutiques, but because of the larger scale of the cities in America, the numbers of people, and the generous amount of space, there were department stores. Every major town in America had two or three big department stores that had started as little mom-and-pop stores, then grown.

When I first started to travel in the 1970s, I saw those stores as they had been for the last twenty years. The families who owned them were very involved in their communities.

They would organize and sponsor events for the communities and often referred to their customers as "patrons." In turn, the people in the communities would work for the stores, buy from the stores, have charge accounts at the stores. The focus was all very local.

The exodus of customers to the suburbs from the city and town centers escalated in the 1970s and started to change the whole retail complexion. The main stores downtown would open one branch in the suburbs, and little by little, as their suburban stores became more profitable, they would open another and another. It was the beginning of the mall. Gradually the downtown areas where the department stores were located began to disintegrate. The weakest of the downtown stores would fall to the strongest, and then they all would vanish. I watched it happen.

But when I first went to those stores, the old-fashioned ways were still in place. I was a rarity, if not a novelty, to the store owners and was treated like a guest of the family. At Stix, Baer and Fuller in St. Louis, for example, I would arrive and be greeted by Mr. Baer. At the end of the day, Mr. Baer would take me to dinner with Mrs. Baer. If I didn't have friends to see or stay with, I would then go to a hotel and, depending on my mood, feel either like lonely Willy Loman on the road or like Eloise at the Plaza having a picnic on my bed.

In cities where I did have friends, the end of the day could be confusing. While I'd been a salesperson working with the customers all day, by night I became a different person. The contrast was particularly extreme during a personal appearance at a mom-and-pop store in Flint, Michigan. In the middle of the day, the store owner asked me kindly if I

had accommodations for the night. When I assured him that I did, that I was staying with friends, he insisted on driving me there. He was a little nonplussed when I directed him to Grosse Pointe, an elite suburb, but when we arrived at the gates of what promised to be an enormous house and I told him I was staying with Henry Ford II and his wife, Christina, he almost had a heart attack.

The evening with the Fords was, in fact, quite odd. I had brought an orange angora caftan for Christina, one of just a few Ferretti had made for me out of extra fabric. During dinner in the coral-colored library, Henry announced that it looked comfortable and put it on. He wore that caftan for the rest of the evening and told me so many times that I should make men's clothes that I got a pounding headache and wished I were staying in a quiet hotel.

In city after city, I would arrive before the stores opened, go in through the staff entrance, and meet the sales-people who would be selling the dresses. By the time the customers arrived for my personal appearance, I would have already shown the entire collection to the sales staff, the different prints, and the groupings of colors for the best display. I would also have been on whatever early-morning local television shows there were and given interviews to the local press. There was tremendous curiosity about this jet-set princess from New York who worked for a living.

From the beginning, almost every reporter asked the same two questions: "Who is your competition?" and "What woman are you designing for?" My answers are almost the same now as they were then. I was not competing with any other designer. No one else was doing what I was. Designer clothes were expensive; mine were not. There was no name

designer at that price level, though it would have been a clever move for any designer to make. But nobody did.

My clothes were flattering to women and not over-whelming. Many designers were men, whose clothes may have shown their creativity but were not always designed to enhance a woman. It was and is so much more important for a woman to be able to express herself rather than expressing a designer's ego.

I have always believed that a woman's clothes should feel like her, be a part of her, and an extension of her personality. That is what I have always liked for myself, and what I liked for myself, I wanted to make for others.

As to the ongoing question about the woman I was designing for, the answer has always been simple: every woman. Taste is ageless. Flirtation and seduction are ageless. Feeling attractive and confident are ageless—and so are women's insecurities.

I talked to women, advised women, listened to women during my tours around the country. Whether in Texas, Georgia, Illinois, or Kansas, we women spoke a common language. "Try this red print or this green print," I urged those who usually wore only brown or navy blue. "I know that's right." I walked through the display racks, helped women with their selections, then often followed them into the changing rooms. "You have to pull the wrap tight in the front so the V neck sits smoothly," I told them. Often I did the pulling myself so the women could see the proper effect. I have thousands of memories of myself looking into changing room mirrors over women's shoulders.

I felt very connected to these women and enjoyed making them look and feel good. Nothing gave me greater

pleasure than seeing a woman transformed by the way she looked in one of my dresses. The mirrors in the dressing rooms were too close, and I encouraged women to look at themselves outside on the sales floor. It was wonderful to see the surprise on their faces and the way their body language changed as they looked at themselves in the mirror. I don't think I know any other designer who actually enjoyed going into the stores the way I did then and do now again. The shyer the customer, the better; the harder the customer, the better. I loved the transformation.

Some buyers were surprised by my instant rapport with their customers, but I took it personally when women passed judgment on the clothes without trying them on. I was so confident about the result that I often chased after women who said they were too old and too fat to wear my dresses. Reluctantly, they would agree to try one on and then would surprise themselves by buying it. This happened all over the country. Women often bought two or three dresses in different prints, then came back and bought more. By the beginning of 1973, the number of my accounts had gone from thirty stores to three hundred.

My business relationship with Ferretti smoothed out quite a bit. I still went to Italy a lot, but the volume of dress orders was enough that he began to focus his factories on making my clothes. My relationship with Egon, however, was not as smooth. We went out too much, everything was a public event. The more I read about "the couple," the more I needed to have an identity of my own.

On the surface, we continued to live a glamorous and

often interesting life between America and Europe. At an elegant dinner in my honor in Houston, I was seated next to astronaut Alan Shepard, the first American in space and one of the few to walk on the moon. I was very impressed to meet someone who had actually seen our planet as a little ball and questioned him endlessly about it. On one of our European trips in the early 1970s, we went to the big ball with a Proust theme in Paris that Marie Hélène de Rothschild hosted as a farewell to the magnificent Château de Ferrières before she closed it. It was an extraordinary sight. The castle was beautifully lit inside and out, and people had made a big effort to dress up. Oscar de la Renta made me a black taffeta dress for the grand occasion, which was photographed by Cecil Beaton. The evening was a true homage to another century, a world that would no longer exist. Another trip took us to Egypt, where in Luxor I felt like Justine discovering the Karnak Temple by moonlight and bought a diaphanous silver antique caftan that I wore to Valentino's couture show in Rome a week later. All was wonderful but there were too many people around us and I felt less and less complicity with my husband.

We also continued to entertain a lot in New York, and our apartment became even more of a mecca for visiting Europeans. One of our friends brought director Bernardo Bertolucci to a party the day after his controversial film *Last Tango in Paris* opened in New York. I loved the movie. Bertolucci was and is a great artist and was very much the man of the moment. I found him as mysterious and arrogant as he was handsome in the red silk Saint Laurent shirt that Marina Schiano had given him that afternoon. We talked politics, not film or fashion, and ended up late at night discussing

democracy and freedom. Like many Italian intellectuals, Bernardo was a Communist, which in America was considered shocking. I found him riveting.

The momentum of my life with Egon covered up the differences that were growing between us, but we didn't discuss them. It all began to unravel at a ball we went to that was organized by Cecil Beaton in Dallas. I wore a Capucci dress with lots of ruffles on the skirt but very little on top. *Newsweek* ran a photograph of Egon and me with barely covered breasts in its Newsmaker section, a photograph that caught the eye of Clay Felker, the editor of *New York* magazine. The cover story he ran about us in *New York* under the headline "The Couple That Has Everything. Is Everything Enough?" forced me to look at our marriage. It did not look good. I was unhappy but rather than complaining about it, I was focusing on work.

Egon admitted publicly to having affairs with other people, which was very painful to me, but I continued to smile and act cool. As a reaction, I started having a secret affair myself. It was my recognition of the loss of intimacy between us, the picture of superficiality that emerged from the story, that forced me to come to terms with the fact that our three-and-a-half-year marriage was over.

When, shortly after the story ran in February 1973, Egon suggested that he get his own apartment, I encouraged him. He and I remained close friends. I never asked him for alimony. I have always resented women asking for alimony if they don't need the money, and by then I had the luxury and the great satisfaction of being able to support myself and my children. Money was never an issue between us.

Besides, it was I who owed so much to him. Not

only had Egon given me the children, the name, and the contacts that had opened so many doors but he had always supported my work and encouraged me. It was he who had insisted on having our children, which, left to my own decision, I might not have done. For that, I'll always be profoundly grateful.

In the years to come, we would always spend Christmas together with the children, and they would often travel with him. At other times, we would travel all together. For the children's sake, I worked hard at keeping the relationship warm and real. I somehow always considered him my husband just as he considered me his wife, though he would remarry after we officially divorced in 1983. To this day he gives me a present for what would have been our anniversary. But, in truth, at the age of twenty-six, I became a single, working mother.

MY LIFE
AS A TYCOON

I BOUGHT CLOUDWALK on December 31, 1974, my twenty-seventh birthday. It was the first major, decisive thing I did on my own after Egon and I separated. It was a statement of my new independence. I felt incredibly proud that I could provide such a luxury for my children and myself.

For the first time I felt I was really taking control of my life and becoming the woman I had always wanted to be. I had two healthy, beautiful children; a cozy apartment in New York; an astonishing country house; a caring boyfriend, Jas Gawronski, the very attractive anchorman for Italian television in New York. I was with Jas on the very first night I bought Cloudwalk. After signing the contract on the afternoon of New Year's Eve, I had gone to the supermarket, bought lamb chops and champagne, and waited for him to drive from the city. Together we celebrated the New Year and camped in my new home. He was loving, providing healing to the wounds I never confessed to having.

My business was skyrocketing. I loved playing the tycooness as I strode through airports wearing fishnet stockings and impossibly high heels with my dresses in a shoulder bag. I was very pleased that I could live a man's life and still be a sexy young woman. I smiled at my shadow.

The dresses continued their meteoric rise, accelerated

in 1974 by the addition of snakeskin and leopard prints to the more conservative geometrics. These came about when three of us were at a meeting in the Seventh Avenue show-room, and we had temporarily run out of inspiration for new prints. "Why not do animal prints? They're always right," I suggested to Dick Conrad and Sue Feinberg, an Italian-speaking American designer I had hired to work with Ferretti in Italy. "Let's do a leopard and a snakeskin. If the whole point of the fabric is that it feels like a second skin, why not make it a real skin?"

The animal prints made their debut in the fall of 1974 at our spring fashion show in the Cotillion Room of the Pierre Hotel. I remember the two-piece snakeskin wrap I wore with pearls while I worked backstage with the models, including Appolonia, a young Dutch girl who would go on to become a top model, and Jerry Hall, a seventeen-year-old girl fresh from Texas who would also become a superstar and marry Mick Jagger. But it was the animal prints that were the stars in 1974.

Three hundred and fifty people came to the show, which I shared with Egon. (He had started a fashion business for men and was showing men's shirts made out of Ferretti's fabric.) Unlike my first show at the Gotham Hotel just two years before, many buyers and a lot of press came because my dresses were selling. And they loved the animal prints, which shortly appeared on the front page of *Women's Wear Daily.*

As the weather warmed up in the late spring and people went outside without their coats, I started seeing the snake and leopard prints on the street. The dresses had lunch at La Grenouille, they walked up and down Madison Avenue,

they were outside the prep schools on the upper East Side, they went into office buildings and out to dinner.

Pepe, my Cuban driver, used to count the snakes and leopards on the street while driving the children to nursery school and report the tally to me at the showroom, where he worked in the stockroom and made shipments. I counted the dresses, too, but for a different reason. It meant that America had accepted me, that I belonged here and was part of the American culture.

I paid little attention to the designers who alternately ignored me or criticized me. I never held myself up as a fabulous designer. I was a woman who made clothes for women. The customers obviously liked them, so did the stores. In the first ten months of 1975, the dresses accounted for more than $14 million in wholesale sales.

I continued to make my rounds of the department stores, more and more of which were carrying my dresses. By 1976, I was up to one thousand stores. My identity had become so interchangeable with the clothes that Rich's department store in Atlanta advertised one of my personal appearances there by displaying a life-sized mannequin of me wearing a green wrap dress. I added new styles to my summer line and used the cotton jersey fabric in pants, tops, jumpsuits, long dresses, and halter-neck dresses. But the little wrap dress remained the all-time favorite. By the end of 1975, I was making fifteen thousand dresses a week.

The business was almost unrecognizable in its transformation. The volume of clothes arriving from Ferretti's factory in Italy was huge, and I had to rent a warehouse on Tenth Avenue to store and ship them. My Seventh Avenue

showroom was jammed with racks of dresses, as were the industrial shelves I'd installed in the stockroom.

The showroom was like a supermarket. So many buyers were coming to the showroom from big stores, little shops, and suburban boutiques that the stock boys had to use shopping carts to fill their orders. The dresses came folded in clear plastic bags, so people could just grab them off the shelves and take them with them.

My dreary solitude in the customs warehouses at Kennedy Airport was long past. By the mid-1970s, the company employed close to one hundred people. There were at least half a dozen salespeople helping Dick Conrad as well as the stockroom people, the warehouse people on Tenth Avenue, the shipping people, and the administrative people.

We expanded abroad to coordinate the dress design and production at Ferretti's factory. Sue Feinberg, having started out working alone in a little office there, hired two assistants to handle the dresses in Italy, so there were three full-time people representing us in Florence.

We also expanded in New York to follow a completely separate and rapidly growing facet of the business: licensing.

MY NAME had suddenly become hot all over the country, which in turn made it a hot property for other people to put on their products. Entrepreneurs in various fields had begun to approach me as early as 1973 to license my name for whatever their specialties were in return for guaranteed minimum fees and a percentage of wholesale sales that ran anywhere from 5 percent to 10 percent.

I didn't even know what licenses were at the time, but most of the contracts we had signed steadily by 1974 proved to be astonishingly successful and lucrative both to the licensees and to us. The licensee paid the high costs of production—the manufacture, warehousing, distribution, and advertising—while the cost to us was limited to design and was far lower.

I worked closely on the design of the products and hired a variety of different people to help me. Among them was one of my best friends, Olivier Gelbsmann, a blue-eyed French stylist I'd met in Geneva, who became my assistant. Another was an American friend named Gail, who had married Cedric Lopez, Egon's best man at our wedding. It was a first job for Gail, who would later become a designer for Ralph Lauren. I also hired an Englishman, Terence, who had an advertising background to oversee publicity and help coordinate the advertising.

There was no room in the Seventh Avenue showroom to add any offices, so I took half a floor in one of those terrifying, high-crime side-street buildings on West Thirty-ninth or Fortieth Street and installed Creative Services there. It wasn't a separate division of the company, just a separate location. Everything was happening so fast, I had to learn as I went along.

One of my first and easiest licenses was with a couple who owned a scarf company. She was the designer and he was the salesman, and they wanted to use the prints I designed for my dresses for silk scarves. I thought it was a great idea. The quality image we were establishing with the dresses was not at risk because we controlled the prints and the fabric they used was a good-quality 100 percent silk. It was also low

maintenance. All I had to do was give them the prints, and they would transform them into interesting scarves. I signed that contract without hesitation.

I also signed a license to do shirts out of Ferretti's fabric with a company named Camicetta, which means "shirt" in Italian. The name was slightly misleading because Camicetta was not an Italian firm but a Seventh Avenue firm. The owner, Harry Ganz, was also much more of a conventional Seventh Avenue wheeler-dealer than the couple who made scarves. But he was very convincing. "You think you're doing well in dresses? If you give me a license, I'll do even more in shirts," he told me. I signed that deal in a rush because he was offering me a good deal of money, but it would turn out to be problematic. Though it was very good financially, the contract with Camicetta would later restrict me from doing a proper sportswear deal with somebody else.

A contract for luggage followed, a deal I signed with a sweet little man with a lisp named Ted Stark. Like the others who had approached me, Ted was a relatively small entrepreneur and very proud of the $30 million luggage business he had built. And his proposition, like that for the scarves and shirts, seemed a good fit with my business. Ted did not want to do conventional suitcases with my name on them; he wanted to start with a line of tote bags, which were a new concept at the time.

I liked the idea of soft, light luggage. I was already carrying my dresses in a shoulder bag when I traveled because they took up so little room and weighed so little, so getting involved with light luggage made sense. I also liked the interesting fabrics Ted showed me for his new luggage, such as nylons and different forms of treated plastics and polyure-

thane, which came in a wide range of colors. The colors were all-important to me: color, after all, was the heart of my dress business.

Purple has always been one of my favorite colors. So I was most pleased one day while I was watching the Muppets on television with the children to see Miss Piggy carrying a purple suitcase. And then I thought, If Miss Piggy has enough confidence to have purple luggage, why shouldn't we offer purple luggage? Ted laughed when I told him. "It will never sell," he said. To Ted's surprise, however, the line of purple totes became huge and, thanks to Miss Piggy, was a best-seller.

I would remain very involved with my luggage license, which I still hold today. The custom jewelry license I signed also made sense. I loved art deco jewelry at the time and had begun to collect antique pieces. I also loved fur coats; everybody did then.

I was delighted when Manny Mohl, the famous fur man in the fur district near Madison Square Garden, said he wanted to do furs with me. I had owned many furs over the years, so I was very happy to put my name on furs and to have my signature on the lining. Manny Mohl also had Bill Blass's name, and I was flattered to have *Diane Von Furstenberg* in such auspicious company.

Other licensing relationships were not as harmonious. I remember distinctly the day Manny Kaye walked into my showroom with a big smile, a cane, and what appeared to be a toupee. Manny, who was a successful entrepreneur in intimate apparel, proposed a line of sleepwear. That seemed fine, and I signed the contract. What I didn't discover until later was that Manny was taking the dresses, having them

duplicated in a cheaper fabric that he was making in Colombia, and then selling them under my name as sleepwear. That was very confusing to the customer, of course, and not at all good for my dress business. I fought hard to make him stop and eventually succeeded. After that episode, we would continue to have a successful association for years to come.

I was also fortunate with an eyewear contract I signed early on and still hold today. Again, it was a young entrepreneur who approached me and this time said, "I want to put your name on eyewear." When I agreed, the young man, whose name was Ed Weiner, and his wife created a company. The company, which they named Optique du Monde and which later licensed Ralph Lauren, did very well. Within the first year it sold something like $5 million worth of *DVF* frames.

Looking back, it is astonishing how quickly the franchises multiplied and how successful they became. The distribution of my dresses was so broad in stores nationwide and the stores were doing so well with the dresses that it was very easy for all the different salesmen of all the different licensed products to place their goods in the stores.

Promoting the various products that carried my name was also easy for the stores and the licensees because of the number of personal appearances I was making. Not only were they sold in the individual departments that carried luggage, scarves, and jewelry, but the stores could incorporate all the products into their windows and their advertising.

The combination took all of us on a very good ride. The licensees who put my name on their products saw their sales skyrocket. The stores that advertised my name sold really well. The huge crowds that came to my personal ap-

pearances didn't buy just the dresses but many other products
with my name on them. The stores benefited, the licensees
benefited, and so, increasingly, did I. By the end of 1975, my
name was on seventeen products and worth some $40 million
in sales.

The early success of the licenses was instructive. It
confirmed the necessity of brand coherence. Because I de-
signed the products, all of which I wore, or worked closely
with the designers I had hired, it was very clear what the
Diane Von Furstenberg image was. It was me. The same
formula seemed to be working in a new business I was
starting at the same time: cosmetics.

I LOVED MAKEUP. Perhaps it was because my mother wouldn't
let me wear any as a young girl. Perhaps it was because my
face has the kind of bone structure that makes it a great face
to make up. Or perhaps it was simply the fashion in the
mid-seventies, when people wore lots of makeup. In any
event, I loved it.

I would buy countless pots and tubes of stage
makeup in different shades and bright colors from a little
store predominantly for stage actors on West Fifty-fifth
Street called the Makeup Center. I loved the theatricality—
the reds, the lavenders, the turquoises. My bathroom in New
York was a pagan altar to the goddess of cosmetics with
offerings of foundation, eye shadows, gels, masks, powders,
rouge, highlighter, eye pencils, lipsticks in pencils, tubes, and
gloss, and mascara, lots and lots of mascara.

Nothing pleased me more than the makeup cere-
mony. I used to sit on the big square sink in my bathroom

with my feet in the basin and my two phones beside me to work on my face in the well-lit mirror. The makeup process was utterly relaxing and creative, but I never thought it would become a business.

On one of my trips in 1973, I forgot my makeup bag. Since I was in a department store, I went into the cosmetics department to buy what I needed. To me, the conventional lines they were selling, such as Elizabeth Arden and Helena Rubinstein, seemed old-fashioned and nothing like the kickier cosmetics I could buy at the Makeup Center. "I should do a makeup line," I thought, and I started to collect all the interesting and unusual colors I could find.

The thought began to turn into reality on a trip I made to Los Angeles later that year. I was very taken by Hollywood at the time, totally starstruck. When Sue Mengers, the Hollywood superagent whom I had met in Rome the summer before, invited me to dinner at Le Bistro with her, her new husband, Jean-Claude Tramont, and actor Ryan O'Neal as my escort, I was thrilled. I had no idea what a force Ryan would be in my professional life.

In 1973, Ryan was very handsome and very hot from his roles in *Love Story* in 1970 and, more recently, in *Paper Moon*. I was a nervous wreck at the thought of having dinner with such a famous superstar and so determined to be as sexy and as thin as possible that I took a diuretic, which I had never done before. During dinner I had to leave the table at least fourteen times to go to the ladies' room, which must have made Ryan think I was either very sick or very strange. Nonetheless, he took me home after dinner to the Beverly Wilshire, where I was staying. And it was there the beauty business was born.

"Why do you need all that stuff?" he said to me after coming upon all the pots and pots of makeup in the bathroom. "I don't need it. I just like it," I told him. But he persisted in that arrogant, condescending way men can have, which in turn made me determined not to be a little, insecure girl who could be pushed around by a movie star. "I didn't buy that makeup for me," I finally answered with an air of superiority. "I'm thinking of buying the company." I was bluffing, of course, but that's when I decided to go into the beauty business, a business that a year later would ring up $2.5 million in sales and ten years later would be sold for over $20 million.

I KNEW ABSOLUTELY nothing about the business of cosmetics, I just loved the idea. So did a French friend of mine, Sylvie Chantecaille, who had just arrived in New York from Paris with her husband and a new baby and was looking for something to do. We talked one afternoon in her apartment on Riverside Drive about the possibility of going into the beauty business together. Sylvie turned out to be interested in skin care, while I was more interested in makeup. "So let's do it," I told her.

It was ridiculous. Sylvie had no experience in cosmetics. I had no experience in cosmetics. We had no plan, no thought of anything concrete. It was mad, all of it. We were venturing into this huge industry on instinct, drive, and nerve.

Sylvie and I visited laboratories and talked to a lot of people with experience. "The money is really in fragrance," they kept saying. I wasn't interested at first. I didn't like most

perfumes. But the words kept coming back—that's where the money was. "You have to create a fragrance," I was told over and over. Having no idea how to do that, I hired somebody who did: Bob Loeb.

There were four or five leading perfume houses, and we met with all of them. These companies buy the essences of flowers and fruits, custom-blend the "notes," as they call them, to create the "juice." You then put the juice into your own packaging, be it perfume, bath oil, or body lotion. Companies such as Firmenich, Roure Du Pont, and IFF (International Flavors & Fragrances) also create flavors for food.

"I want something that simply smells good, like cut fresh flowers, a scent you can inhale and almost swallow, like you can with the smell of a roasting chicken," I told people at the different companies, whose perfumers are called "noses." "I don't want something that smells like your grandmother's handkerchief."

I understood what I meant, but the chemists and noses did not. The poor account executives kept bringing new notes in various combinations to our office. But they were always too heavy, too obvious, too reminiscent of another fragrance or another time.

I tried words such as "alive," "up," and "open" and urged them to use only white flowers such as jasmine, honeysuckle, lilac, hyacinth, gardenia. But not gardenias in full flower; young, green gardenias had the lighter, fresher scent I was looking for. But nothing came of my efforts. After I had sniffed and worn and rejected a hundred or so samples, we were stalemated.

It was Bob Loeb who broke the stalemate. He invited

the head nose at Roure Du Pont to the fashion show for the spring collection at the Pierre Hotel in 1974. Jim Bell, a tall, attractive, athletic man who looked like a basketball player, saw the clothes on the models, saw the way the models moved in the clothes, saw the way they interacted with the male models they had on their arms, and finally understood the spirit I was trying to convey. The next batch of samples from Roure Du Pont contained what seemed to be a winner —light, airy, sensual. I wore it and got lots of compliments. Finally, we had the scent. Now we had to name it.

Our entire cosmetics division, which consisted of Bob, Sylvie, her assistant Lydia, and me, was working out of the library in my apartment. My three-year-old daughter wandered in during one of our sessions, looking mischievous as ever with her green cat's eyes, and there it was. "Why don't we call the fragrance *Tatiana?*" Bob suggested. An image flashed through my mind of Tatiana at Cloudwalk mashing lilac flowers and water in a coffee can to make a child's version of perfume. *Tatiana.* Perfect. We had the name of the scent—now to launch it.

The traditional way of launching a new scent was and is a very expensive proposition. It requires heavy advertising to create an image and an established sales force to cover the stores. Halston, who was launching his fragrance at the same time, was being underwritten by Norton Simon and could afford both. We could not.

I can't remember which of us came up with the solution, but it was brilliant. I was selling thousands of dresses a week to stores throughout the country. Why not attach a packet of *Tatiana* to the washing instructions in each dress and get the scent sampled all over the country for free?

And that is how we launched the perfume so widely and successfully in 1975.

DIANE At the same time, I was working with Sylvie on the cosmetics line. While she was developing the formulas, I was working on the colors. The problem was, how to distribute the cosmetics line?

I decided, without thinking much about it, to create a small beauty store, more or less my own version of the Makeup Center. Real estate on Madison Avenue was not very expensive at the time so I rented a small boutique between Sixtieth and Sixty-first Streets. At first it was the only place the cosmetics were sold. I was a dress designer, after all, and the cosmetics were just an amusing sideline.

I decorated the boutique in beige tones, vaguely inspired by the perfume house of Guerlain on the Champs-Élysées in Paris. I also chose a shade of beige for the plastic components of the cosmetics—the compacts for the lipsticks, the eye liners, the powders. The packaging I designed for the first boxes of *Tatiana* was a taupe, gray, and white geometric pattern, as was the carpeting in the salon. It resembled the prints for my dresses.

The front of the salon had four little bars and stools with testers where women could play with makeup. In the back there was a professional makeup artist, who would offer women complete makeovers. To store the products I found eight antique mirrors with women representing the four seasons painted on them, and had them made into cabinets. It all looked very inviting.

For the opening of the salon in 1975, I took a full-page ad in *The New York Times*, hired a professional copywriter to write the copy, and had my photograph taken by Fran-

cesco Scavullo. Scavullo was an old friend from the first days when I had stayed with Egon in New York before we married and had been the first major photographer to shoot me when I was contemplating becoming a model. I didn't particularly love the way I looked in the announcement ad for the beauty boutique, but looking back now, of course, any photograph taken at that age looks beautiful.

Ryan O'Neal would have been horrified at all the makeup being sold to so many women. But the women who came in not knowing how best to use makeup and, after a session with the makeup artist or me, walked out with a personalized makeup chart and lots of products loved it. And so did I.

I kept expenses down by using only stock packaging and stock bottles. I didn't have anything made, unlike Halston, who commissioned Elsa Peretti to design her trademark lopsided bottle for his scent and create a special mold for the bottle. We sold *Tatiana* in a stock spray like many other moderately priced sprays.

I wanted to grow slowly and at first resisted the offer from Bloomingdale's legendary "Mr. Cosmetics," Mike Blumenfeld, to open my own counter in Bloomingdale's. Once I got into the stores, I would have to support the line with salespeople and advertising, and I was afraid it would be too much to handle.

In 1976, I relented. The line was going so well, I felt secure enough to launch it nationally. It made good business sense for customers sampling *Tatiana* on my dresses to be able to buy the scent at department store perfume counters and to try my beauty products at the cosmetics counter Mike per-

suaded me to open. To coincide with the national launch, I wrote a book for Simon & Schuster titled *Diane Von Furstenberg's Book of Beauty* and went on a national tour to promote both the book and the cosmetics.

What a blast we had on the road. I took with me Gigi Williams, a very slim, very funky-looking girl who was living with Ronnie Cutrone, an artist who assisted Andy Warhol and was part of the Factory family. Like me, Gigi was very much into the glamorous movie stars of the forties and fifties, such as Marlene Dietrich, Dorothy Lamour, and Lauren Bacall. Our days on the road were hardly glamorous, however.

We often started at 6 A.M. if we had television interviews, then went on to do morning makeup sessions at the downtown store of whatever city we were in, followed by two or three suburban branches in the afternoon. It was exhausting being on our feet all day, especially on our very high heels. We let off steam in the limousines the stores sent us around in. Dark, one-way glass had just become the vogue and Gigi and I would put our feet up and fantasize that we were two hot chicks on a rock-and-roll tour. We laughed a lot but we also worked hard.

My dream was to join the ranks of women like Helena Rubinstein, Elizabeth Arden, and Estée Lauder, who had pioneered the cosmetics industry and created their own empires. I loved the legends of these women and rather fancied myself as an up-and-coming one of them. Incredibly, the dream appeared to be within reach. By the end of 1975, the combined retail sales from my clothes, my licenses, and my new fragrance and cosmetics line was $60 million. I was twenty-eight years old.

□

When I first started out in business, I projected a vision of myself by thirty as a glamorous, successful woman stepping into and out of limousines and planes, sweeping into movie and theater openings past a phalanx of photographers, toying with the attentions of equally glamorous men. In that vision, I was a woman who felt free with her life, free with her affections, free from conventions and restrictions. And there is no question that I fulfilled that dream and even went beyond it.

One of my ambitions in the early years of my career was to be on the cover of *Fortune* magazine. In 1976, I happily settled for a front-page story in *The Wall Street Journal* about what the paper called my "fashion empire." I'll never forget the satisfaction I felt on January 28, the day the story ran. I was reading it on an early-morning plane to Cleveland, dressed as usual in one of my loosely buttoned shirtdresses with a lot of leg showing. "What's a pretty girl like you doing reading *The Wall Street Journal?*" my male seat companion asked, trying to start a conversation. It was Ryan O'Neal all over again, but this time I didn't even bother to respond. I smiled at him, thought "jerk," and returned to reading the paper. I knew who I was and what I had accomplished. He wasn't on the front page of *The Wall Street Journal.* I was.

Things only got better. Two months later, I was on the cover of *Newsweek.* I couldn't believe the serious attention I and my business were being given only three years after I had been trashed as a dilettante in *New York* magazine. But there I was on a magazine cover on every newsstand on five continents: a European girl living the American dream.

I had no idea at the time how the cover story would change my life. I had no idea in the week before the March 22, 1976, issue, in fact, that I was even going to be on the cover. Though I obviously knew *Newsweek* was doing a story about me, the cover was supposed to be Gerald Ford, who had just won his first Republican presidential primary that week. Even when *Newsweek* called me urgently at the office toward the end of the week and told me I had to have a cover picture taken just in case, it didn't occur to me that I would be chosen over the president of the United States.

Newsweek arranged to have my photograph taken at the last minute by Scavullo, who was in the midst of shooting a cover for *Cosmopolitan* magazine. There was no time for me to prepare, so I simply grabbed a green shirtdress off the rack and one of my falls (straightening my curly hair made it look thin, and the falls made it look longer and thicker). I arrived alone at Scavullo's carriage house on East Sixty-third Street. It was almost as if I was having my passport picture taken. Scavullo was far better prepared for the cover shoot than I was. The famous makeup artist Way Bandy was already there for the *Cosmo* shoot, as was François, a young Swiss hairdresser, so they got me ready. And the photo ran on the cover.

I'd like to think that I got the cover because I was a better story than Gerald Ford, but that would be naive. I have long since learned that journalists do not write about you to make you happy or because they are necessarily even interested in you, but because you are a good story. It was March, the month in which the newsweeklies are rated by their newsstand sales. If the editors put a sexy girl on the cover, they sell more magazines. Just as you sell products, you

become a product yourself. And that was fine with me. It was good for *Newsweek*, and it was great for me.

The cover proved to be extremely validating. I had a full schedule already planned for the week the issue ran, including a personal appearance in Toronto. I was so used to doing personal appearances all over America that it did not occur to me that I would need my passport. The Canadian immigration authorities at the airport refused to admit me until I thought to show them the cover story in *Newsweek*. "Will this prove to you who I am?" I asked them half joking, half apologizing. They let me in.

The *Newsweek* cover also coincided with my first trip to the White House. I had been invited to a dinner there the month before by Louis Estevez, the California designer who made clothes for Betty Ford. I was very impressed and nervous about going to the White House and I called Halston and borrowed a strapless black dress from him. The White House is the quintessence of a beautiful American building, functional, simple, and elegant. But it is quite modest when you realize that it represents the center of the world's power. I had to pinch myself as I walked through the reception rooms.

I was even more nervous when I discovered that I was seated at the president's table. Though I acted very cool on the outside, inside I was a young, wide-eyed Belgian girl who couldn't believe she was at the White House. Even more unsettling was the realization that everyone knew who I was.

The *Newsweek* cover had made me into a national figure, and I was not prepared. It had all happened so fast that I hadn't had time to absorb it. Unbelievably, I found myself bantering with the president of the United States about beating him out for the cover. "The editors didn't

know until Saturday whether it was you or me," I said half apologetically, to which he responded gallantly, "If I had to be beaten by anyone, I'm glad it was you." President Ford was a very likable, reassuring figure. He had had the difficult task of taking over the presidency after Nixon's resignation, and he was almost like a Band-Aid for the wounded country. His wife, Betty, was wonderfully open and full of life.

The evening passed in a blur, especially when President Ford asked me to dance. It was a fox-trot or some old-fashioned dance like that which I absolutely could not do at all. He was a very good dancer, but all I did was trip over his feet and pray the dance would end before my strapless dress fell off.

The most impressive memory of that evening did not involve the president, however, but his secretary of state, Henry Kissinger. There was no more recognizable person on earth at that time than Henry Kissinger, yet he too knew who I was and actually introduced himself to me. "We were talking about you with the pilots flying into Washington this afternoon and looking at your picture on the cover of *Newsweek*," he said to me in his thick accent. I was completely taken aback and of course flattered. He was charming, and he knew it.

Henry and I became good friends. He and his wife, Nancy, moved near me in Connecticut, and I frequently had Thanksgiving dinner with them. Over the years, I would often lunch alone with Henry, which is, for me, like eating with a living history book. Our political inclinations, however, have always gone in opposite directions.

I was more in tune with politically liberal thinkers and, specifically in 1976, with Jerry Brown, who was running

for the Democratic presidential nomination. Jerry had made a great impression on me when I'd met him in California, so I volunteered to help him. To my own surprise I found myself hosting a party in New York City to introduce him to influential New Yorkers, such as Barbara Walters, Diana Ross, and Felix Rohatyn, the investment banker who was trying to save the city from bankruptcy. The next morning my name was on the front page of *The New York Times*.

It seems as extraordinary to me now as it did then that I had enough poise and self-assurance as a twenty-nine-year-old foreign girl to introduce a candidate for the presidency to these New York luminaries. But I was very drawn to Jerry. Not only did I find him extremely attractive, I was very intrigued by his life, which had led him from Berkeley radical to Jesuit seminarian to the governor of California.

Jerry and I became friends, and I continued to see him, often in New York. He was always looking for a room for himself or his traveling campaign apparatus, and his main contacts in New York were the writer Joan Didion and I. I saw him in California as well. One memorable evening I drove him to his house in Laurel Canyon after dinner. I wonder what his security people would have thought if they had known I didn't have a driver's license then. I also went with him to the Democratic National Convention in New York. As he counted his votes, I counted the number of my dresses on the delegates. I may have had more dresses than he had votes.

My personal relationship with Jerry was never more than a flirtation, really. Besides, by the time of the Democratic convention in 1976, I was very involved with a man who would become central to my life: Barry Diller.

I had met Barry the year before at a party I was giving in New York for Sue Mengers, my Hollywood friend who had set me up with Ryan O'Neal two years before. She asked me if she could bring Barry Diller to the party, and of course I said yes. I was very excited to meet the new thirty-three-year-old chairman of Paramount Pictures. The movie business had always been very appealing to me, and Barry was a shaker in the movie industry.

I knew that Barry had the reputation of being tough, shy, and hard to get to know, so I was somewhat surprised when we immediately connected and established what seemed to be an instant rapport. "How nice," I remember thinking. "It will be so much fun to have Barry as a friend." I certainly didn't think we were going to fall in love.

Barry called me from Los Angeles soon after the party and asked me to have dinner. The only problem, he explained in his brusque way, was that he didn't know much about restaurants in New York. When he came to pick me up, I suggested that instead of going out to a noisy restaurant, we could stay in. I had had dinner prepared in my apartment. There was electricity in the air, and I knew, we both knew, that we were going to be more than just friends.

Barry kept on calling me and we spoke daily, a routine that exists to this day. The following week when I went to Paris, he continued to call me there. Finally, he said, "Why don't you just come to Los Angeles?" Without hesitation, I said, "I'll be there tomorrow." And I took a flight, seventeen hours, from Paris to L.A. I was so excited, I could have flown there on my own wings.

I loved the adventure of flying halfway around the

world into the unknown. At a stopover in Canada where I had to change planes, I called Jas, my journalist boyfriend, mumbled a few words, and told him I was flying to Califor- nia to meet someone else. We had kept our relationship at arm's length. Although separated from his wife, he was married. And as for me, my children and my career were my priorities. The reality of the adventure, however, was unnerving. As the plane approached Los Angeles, I got more and more agitated. When the pilots announced we were over Phoenix, I locked myself in the bathroom and stayed there until five minutes before we landed, washing myself, perfuming myself, putting on makeup, changing my clothes from a comfortable dress into a blue pin-striped pantsuit that had the look—and only the look—of the perfect traveling gear.

Barry was probably just as nervous, but I was such a wreck when I arrived at the airport that I didn't notice. All I saw was Barry looking very handsome and glamorous in a yellow E-type Jaguar with a limousine for the luggage to follow. His house in Beverly Hills was just as glamorous, filled with natural light from skylights and huge windows, and the guest room he had prepared for me was filled with fresh flowers. I hung my clothes in the guest room, but I didn't sleep there that night—or, indeed, ever. Very soon after he gave up his apartment in New York and lived with us when he was not in California.

Our relationship was unique from day one and quite unexplainable. I fell very much in love with Barry, and I was overwhelmed by the way he loved me. Barry totally gave into me, trusted me blindly, and loved me unconditionally. Later I would have other people in my heart and in my life, but

somehow Barry was always there. Never, ever, even for a second, under any circumstances, has he not been there for me. And that's pretty amazing.

There was passion between us; love, support, honesty. There was never anything at all forced between us. I have never had to lie to him, never ever. Though I don't lie in the normal course of events, Barry made it even easier for me. Long term, that made him much stronger and so much more important in my life. The way he loves me is true and unique.

The existence of Barry in my life and the quality and intensity of his love would give me a lot of freedom, maybe too much, and would often intimidate and restrain other people in my life. We would be closer at some times than at others. But though our relationship would change, its quality did not. No matter what happened over the years, neither one of us would ever let anything affect the bond between us.

Marriage to Barry, or to any man for that matter, was never a goal. Perhaps it is because I have such idealized expectations of a perfect union and I am terrified of being disappointed. I prefer to think of a relationship as a daily choice or at least that is what I preach. I consider it a privilege to be able to support my lifestyle and my family myself. It is indeed a true luxury to feel free to enjoy the company of men for the pure pleasure of it. I could then accept their love and gifts, such as the twenty-nine loose diamonds in a Band-Aid box Barry gave me on my twenty-ninth birthday or the album of photographs he commissioned to be taken of every newsstand in the five boroughs of New York the week I was on the cover of *Newsweek*.

□

BARRY CHARTERED a big sailboat in 1976 to watch the Bicentennial fireworks in New York Harbor and invited a lot of our friends. I felt very American as my American children and I watched the Brooklyn Bridge lit up by the fireworks. The next year he joined me in Japan, where I was making personal appearances for the first time in stores such as Seibu and Isetan. We went on to Hong Kong for an incredible weekend.

"What are we going to do?" we asked each other. I looked at a map and saw that the closest interesting place we could go was the Philippines. And that gave me an idea. I had met Imelda Marcos, the first lady of the Philippines, at Trader Vic's the year before at a dinner with Lee Radziwill and Andy Warhol. Andy had wanted to produce two princesses for Mrs. Marcos, and Lee, who had been married to Prince Stanislaus Radziwill, and I were the only two he could find in New York.

I hadn't been particularly impressed or unimpressed with Mrs. Marcos. She was a handsome woman and larger than life in every way. She exuded a sense of self-importance and boasted about the time she had spent with Mao Tsetung and Richard Nixon. She thought of herself as a bridge between China and America. *Tatiana,* my perfume, was her favorite fragrance, she told me, because it reminded her of ylang-ylang, the flower of her country. At the end of the evening, she had invited all of us to come visit her in the Philippines, a fairly safe invitation while we were all sitting in New York. But here Barry and I were in Hong Kong along with my good friend Olivier.

"Why don't we call Mrs. Marcos?" I said. I picked up the phone and half jokingly asked the operator to get me the palace in the Philippines. To my amazement, fifteen minutes later I got a call back. It was not Mrs. Marcos, who I was told, was in Libya consulting Mu'ammar Gadhafi about problems she was having with Muslims in her country, but a friend of hers, Mrs. Tantoco, who owned a department store in Manila that carried my dresses and *Tatiana.* Mrs. Tantoco invited us on behalf of Mrs. Marcos to be presidential guests for the weekend.

The sirens on our police escort from the airport made little impression on the traffic in Manila, but the beautiful architecture of the Presidential Palace made a great impression on us. So did the guest house we were shown to, which was filled with thousands of flowers and, what seemed, just as many servants. It was a blast. Everything in the country was at our disposal, Mrs. Tantoco told us, whatever we wanted to do for two days.

The next day, after we visited her department store and bought many Philippine crafts, the three of us flew out over a series of beautiful rapids, where I started to photograph what appeared to be old ruins. "What are they, where are the ruins from?" I asked, thinking it was some ancient culture. "Oh, those are from the movie set for *Apocalypse Now,*" came the response. "Why don't we go and visit Francis?" Barry said, referring to Francis Ford Coppola, the film's director.

We took a helicopter to the mountains the next day, and all of a sudden it was as if we were in the middle of the Vietnam War. There were hundreds of GIs carrying guns and wearing camouflage and hundreds of North Vietnamese

doing the same thing. It was a glimpse of hell. But what an amazing, formidable man Francis turned out to be. He dealt with hell all day, was totally passionate about the movie and lived in paradise in this beautiful place called Seven Pools. We drank hot cocoa ground from beans taken straight from the trees and swam in the natural pools of different temperatures around his house against a backdrop of mountains of flowers and palm trees. It was an afternoon filled with such contrasts that I will never forget it. It alone was worth the trip. What I later read in the news about the corruption in the Philippines made me feel somewhat guilty that I had accepted the invitation but I cherish the memories of those few days.

Peace, not war, would bring me to the White House again in 1979 with Barry to celebrate the signing of the Camp David Peace Accord. President Jimmy Carter looked very content, and rightfully so, sitting with the Begins and the Sadats at Table A. Seeing the Egyptians and the Israelis together after so many years of enmity was extraordinary, and uplifting to me anyway. Yitzhak Shamir, then speaker of the Knesset and future prime minister, my dinner partner in the Rose Garden, was not happy about the Peace Accord and kept insisting that there could never be peace with the Arabs. I would have argued more strenuously if I hadn't been so cold.

Vice President Walter Mondale, at whose table I was seated, saw me shivering and asked a Secret Service agent to lend me his raincoat. Then I felt better. There was nothing anyone could do however, about the terminal damage done to my new Manolo Blahnik shoes by the wet White House lawn, but I didn't care. It was a fabulous evening, a privilege

to be present at this historical moment, especially with such a great seat at Table B. Then, as usual, Barry and I went back to our separate lives on our respective coasts. Barry had his work to do. And I, increasingly, had mine.

SHORTLY AFTER the *Newsweek* story, I was approached by a bedspread manufacturer, who offered me a huge advance just to put my name on the bedspreads he was making for Sears, Roebuck. That made me think that if he was willing to give me that much just for a bedspread, why not do the whole house?

I had become intrigued with Sears and its involvement in home design. Every woman's magazine I read as I flew around the country seemed to have at least six advertising pages devoted to what I considered to be Sears' dull designs for their unattractive little houses. If Sears was investing so heavily in home design, why not make pretty homes? And why shouldn't I do it? I was dressing so many American women, I reasoned, I might as well design their homes.

Home design seemed a natural extension of what I was already doing, and Sears, with its millions of loyal customers, was a challenge. I had no idea at the time of the caste system within the retail business that relegated Sears below department stores. I didn't even know that Sears was not considered a department store. To me, Sears was a huge store that had a catalog that was as familiar to the American home as the Bible. My only concern was finding out the name of the person to contact at Sears.

□

PERHAPS CHARLES MORAN, the head of Sears' home furnishings department, agreed to see me because his wife wore my dresses. Or perhaps he knew I was successful because of all the publicity I was getting. But it was I who was definitely in awe of him. Charles Moran was a very important merchant in a very big industry and responsible, at that time, for more than $1 billion a year in sales. Every person with something to sell must have tried to court him, because he had more buying power than anyone else in the home furnishings business.

I flew to Chicago by myself one summer morning and walked nonchalantly into a boardroom in the very impressive Sears Tower, then the tallest building in the world. The dozen or so people at the meeting seemed pretty old to me, almost every one of them a middle-aged midwestern man in a polyester suit. I must have seemed like an alien to them in this heart of the American heartland—an exotic-looking woman from New York with a foreign accent, a flowered dress, and masses of long, curly hair.

I had been tricked into letting my hair go curly by Ara Gallant, a photographer in New York. Ara had been shooting me late at night (he preferred to work at night) for the cover of Andy Warhol's magazine, *Interview*, when he told me to wet my hair. I was shocked. I had built my security around having straight hair, and wetting it would make it curly. But Ara, a strange man who walked like a cat, dressed all in black, and had hundreds of gold charms on his cap, assured me he had already taken the shot for the cover. As my hair started to dry into the natural ringlets I had always hated, Ara took a pair of scissors, made jagged cuts in my body suit, and started shooting again. The result was a dramatic, wonderful, unusual photograph that ended up on the

cover of *Interview*. From that day on, for almost fifteen years, I would let my hair stay curly. I felt freer than ever.

DIANE I don't think the men at Sears had ever done business with a woman before, especially one who looked like me. There were very few businesswomen at the time, and the few in management tended to play down their gender by dressing more like men than like women. For me, however, flaunting my femininity had always given me an advantage, even a weapon. It gave me the opportunity to charm, to be light and fun and seductive. That awkward morning at Sears, the men didn't know whether to stand up or remain seated when I came into the meeting room.

"Well, what do you think you could do for us?" Moran asked me. I replied that I considered myself a successful designer, albeit in dresses and not home furnishings. "I'm selling over fifteen thousand dresses a week and dressing so many women in America that I would welcome the challenge of designing American homes," I told him. I showed him some sketches of sheets and home accessories I had put together in a book. Nobody said a thing.

"What kind of compensation would you like to get?" Moran asked. Emboldened by the big figure I'd been offered by the bedspread person, I responded, "Well, the compensation would be based on royalties on sales, but in any case I would not do it for less than a guarantee of half a million dollars." Again nobody said anything and I soon left.

Looking back, I realize how young and arrogant I was. Who did I think I was, asking for a huge sum? It was probably more than any of the men in that room were making at Sears, and I was half their age. But the thought never occurred to me. I flew back to New York and talked with

Charles Moran several times over the phone. Nothing happened. The tide turned a month or so later, when I returned to Chicago for a personal appearance at Marshall Field's and called Moran from a pay phone at the store. To my astonishment, he told me we had a deal.

The arrangement was indeed unique. The other license contracts I held were with manufacturers. With Sears, the deal I made was directly with a big retailer for what was essentially a private-label line and much like the concept I would propose to Federated Department Stores twenty years later. *The Diane Von Furstenberg Style for Living Collection*, as the line for Sears came to be called, would be sold exclusively in Sears stores across the country. Thus began my seven-year relationship with Charles Moran and his successor, John Easter, who became a friend. Those would be some of the most instructive and lucrative years of my business life.

THERE WAS TOO MUCH going on at the showroom on Seventh Avenue to handle the Sears account, so I set up a design studio in my apartment and hired a designer named Marita. We started very small, just as I had with the dresses and the cosmetics. Our first product was sheets. I painted the pattern myself, helped by Marita (an old-fashioned bouquet of flowers bordering an overall pattern of little white flowers on a ground of pale blue), and called it Carnation Bouquet. It turned out to be a very successful pattern and soon appeared on John Travolta's bed in the film *Urban Cowboy*. It also paved the way for an ever-broadening range of color-coordinated products under my name for Sears.

Towels. Curtains. Tableware. Rugs. Everything for

the bed, bath, table, and home would follow. Four times a year we would introduce a new collection or slightly alter an existing one, always making sure that the design was coordinated with the prior products. (Years later, I would use that same concept in clothes by building a coordinated wardrobe piece by piece in the line I sell on television.)

Designing furniture for Sears was harder. The textiles in the sheets and towels could be tied together and varied by color, which the furniture couldn't. The furniture people were also harder to work with. They didn't feel I had the qualifications to design furniture. But I learned from them as well.

As the Sears business grew and I became involved in designing more and more products, I hired more designers to help cover the account, including Peter and Christine D'Ascoli, a talented couple who took charge of the Sears collection. We worked directly with the Sears suppliers and then presented our product designs to the Sears buyers, each of whom was supposed to carry one or more *DVF Style for Living* design in his respective category. It was an exhausting process. Every product line had at least two or three buyers. Curtains alone had five.

It took three or four days every three months or so and long meetings at Sears in Chicago for us to present each of our products to the buyers in each specific category. Every half hour, a different set of Sears buyers would cycle through the austere room we sat in. At the end of the day, I would be ready to get drunk or do anything just to get out of there.

The experience with Sears was invaluable, however, and it gave me a tremendous education in the home furnishings industry. The suppliers opened all their technology to us

and showed us everything they could do. Because Sears had such a "big pencil" (industry jargon for large orders), the suppliers knew that if I chose a product from their line for my designs or helped them create a product, they would end up with a big order. As a result, the suppliers were always welcoming to me, and I learned a lot from each of them.

There was one major drawback to working with Sears, which I hadn't really been aware of when I signed the license deal. In the often unforgiving retail hierarchy, it was unheard of for a designer to sell to both upper-tier stores such as Saks, Bloomingdale's, and Neiman Marcus and a mass merchant such as Sears. Partly because I was so successful with the products I had in department store distribution, however, and partly because I could justify the hard goods side of home products as being entirely different from my apparel and cosmetics, I managed to get away with it.

My relationship with Sears was wonderful. In the seven years I would work with them, retail sales of my home furnishings line went from $35 million a year to $100 million.

My life was hectic, and Cloudwalk was my major source of sanity. I don't think I could have survived without it. I needed quiet and space, and I spent as much time as I could there with the children. I cooked on weekends, cleaned up the children's milk-logged Rice Krispies from the table in the television room, and took long walks through the woods with Alexandre; Tatiana being more of an indoor, city girl at the time.

At first the roof in the main house at Cloudwalk leaked. So did the glass in the old windows, as evidenced by

the huge heating bills. But I didn't care. There wasn't a day that passed at Cloudwalk, nor is there now, that I didn't look around me and thank the little dress.

Four days a week I lived the life of a tycoon, designing and negotiating, jetting around the country and to Italy to see Ferretti. Every morning started with calls on one of my home phone lines to the factory in Como, calls on the other line to and from department stores, suppliers, and lawyers, calls on the tie-line to my office. Every night I tried to be home at dinnertime with the children before spending the hours until midnight on the phones to California, to Asia, and to Japan, where my dresses were selling very well. And then came Thursday.

Every Thursday night, without fail, I drove to Cloudwalk. Often I was not alone. Romance and physical love were wonderful diversions and reaffirming. From Monday to Thursday I lived the life of a man. On Thursday nights at Cloudwalk I could indulge myself in being a needy woman.

Friday belonged to me. Inevitably there were loose business ends to clean up, but I guarded the time I had for myself jealously. I took walks and long baths. I read. My companion would leave before the children arrived after school on Friday, and I would devote myself to them for the rest of the weekend.

Cloudwalk was a paradise for children, and often Tatiana and Alexandre would bring their friends from New York. They could each bring a maximum of three, and though I often had friends for the weekend, I spent many weekends alone with four or five kids. They were on their own during the day, but I cooked our meals and we all

gathered loudly around the table to eat together. At least once a month, it seemed, I ended up in the emergency room of the local hospital with one child or another who had a splinter I couldn't get out or a cut that might need stitches.

People often asked me how I could work so hard and raise a family at the same time, but to me it was natural, it was simply what I did. I was less certain about whether I could have combined a husband, business, and children. The truth of the matter is that if I'd stayed married, I don't think I would have been such an attentive mother. Being a single mother made my relationship with my children more essential and maybe easier.

I shared everything with my children and they with me. At the end of every day we would have what we called "discussion time" on their beds, where we exchanged news on what we had done at school and at work, respectively. I involved them in every facet of my business and often brought home packaging and other things I was working on to show them. Their reaction was often enlightening.

I remember the night I brought home samples of the new *Tatiana* bath line, and little Tatiana, who was maybe seven, looked at the talcum powder in its plastic container and said, "If you put it in a box, you could charge more money." She gave me equally good advice when I was doing sheets for the Sears line and moved from printed sheets and towels to solids. It was Tatiana, who was ten at the most, who came up with the name "Sensational Solids." The children took a great interest in my business. On the way home from school, they used to stop at Gimbel's East on the corner of Eighty-sixth Street to check the cosmetics counter and then report to me.

I always treated my children and their friends as equals and never patronized them, though I was strict about certain things. I hate guns, and I never let the children play with them. When Alexandre would sneak a toy gun into the house, I would immediately take it away. I had a large collection of confiscated toy guns in the medicine chest in my bathroom.

I didn't want them to watch violent movies either, or movies that I thought would disturb them. Barry had a screening room installed in the old tobacco barn-turned-studio at Cloudwalk, and I remember one day forbidding the children to watch *Kramer vs. Kramer*. The film was about the children of divorce, and I thought it might upset them. Tatiana was furious and protested the decision by organizing a demonstration with her brother and picketing with signs outside the barn. I finally gave in on that one but held firm on *Marathon Man*. The film was being shown on Charlie Bluhdorn's private Gulf Stream, which was flying Barry, Michael Eisner, and me and the children to New York from Santo Domingo, and I forced my children to spend the entire time locked in the bathroom. It is one of their favorite childhood stories now, although they did not appreciate it then.

I never had any doubt about how to raise them. The fact that my mother was always present in the house was, of course, a major help. She would play backgammon with my son, speak French to my daughter, and often be a buffer if we needed one. They adored her and still do. She and Tatiana speak every day on the phone, and Alexandre loves to take her to lunch and sometimes to a basketball game.

The only part of raising children that truly intimi-

Newspaper clippings of famous women wearing the wrap dress in 1976: Gloria
Steinem, Betty Ford, Julie Nixon Eisenhower, an unidentified blonde with Henry
Kissinger, Maureen Dean (Watergate scandal), and Dina Merrill.

At work in the showroom. *(Burt Glinn, Magnum Photos)*

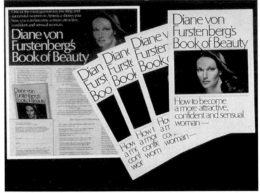

Developing my cosmetics line taught me so much about makeup and various beauty tricks that I decided to write the *Book of Beauty*.

On the road, meeting customers and doing makeovers. *(S. Karin Epstein, Camera 5)*

For my Fall 1978 fashion show, the illustrator Michael Vollbrach made masks with my face on them for the models. I was surrounded by Iman and a very young Janice Dickinson, who had just started modeling. *(Pierre Scherman, WWD)*

On the cover of *Interview*. My friend Ara Gallant shot this photo of me with wet hair late one night. I liked it so much that I decided to wear my hair curly from then on.
(Ara Gallant, Interview*)*

Albert Watson took this picture of me on election day 1980; the day Ronald Reagan was elected president. *(Albert Watson)*

Gia was the most beautiful girl I had ever seen. The photographer Chris von Wangenheim shot this ad campaign for me. They both died tragically a few years later. *(Chris von Wangenheim)*

The view of the apple orchard at Cloudwalk: my home, my refuge, and the key to my sanity. *(Stewart O'Shields)*

Tatiana and Alexandre, at ages eight and nine, respectively. The two of them were always together. I took them everywhere with me and always listened to their opinions.

Reunited with my father, mother, and brother at Le Zoute, the seaside resort in Belgium.

Summer 1978 in Deauville, France, with Barry and the children. I brought my American family to Deauville, where I used to go on weekends when I lived in Paris. I irritated them because I spoke French, they irritated me because they didn't; but we had a great time anyway.

Always on the go . . . an early ad for a luggage licensee.

Even though I wasn't really posing on the Empire State Building, this was the most painful position I had ever been photographed in. This ad was one in a series for a Japanese jeans licensee.

Friends Olivier Gelbsmann and André Leon Talley in my Fifth Avenue office.

With Gloria Steinem, Bella Abzug, and Barbra Streisand at a benefit for the feminist group, Women USA. *(David McGough/DMI)*

With Raquel Welch and Diana Ross at a benefit for the Costume Institute of the Metropolitan Museum of Art in New York. (Daily News)

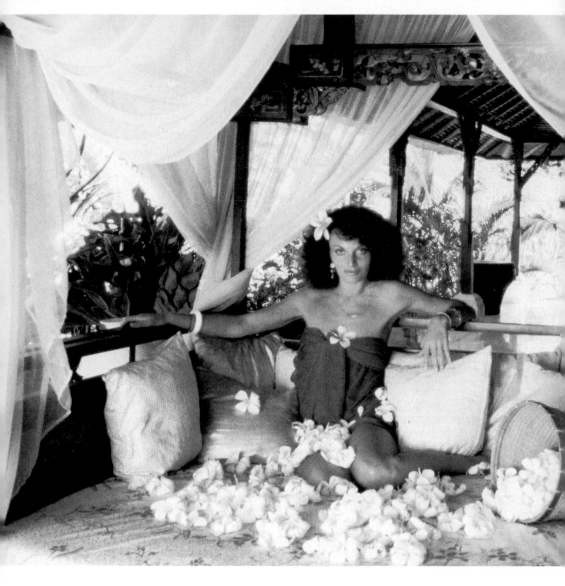

Sitting on a Balinese bed among the frangipani blossoms in Bali, a place of great inspiration to me.

OPPOSITE:
TOP: The Balinese ceremonial flags I brought to Cloudwalk in 1980. The flags have stood there ever since. As they weather, I replace them and change the colors.

BOTTOM: Brazilian Paulo Fernandes in Bali. Paulo lived in a bamboo house and was a collector and dealer of furniture, art, and textiles. He was calm and easy-going: a big change from my hectic New York life.

The *Volcan d'Amour* creative team at the launch party: Dakota Jackson (designed the bottle), Antonio Piticov (conceived the packaging), Paulo (I dedicated the fragrance to him), Janet Chin Jay (managed the product), Susan Garry (wrote the copy), and Michael Smith.

BELOW LEFT: The *Volcan d'Amour* (volcano of love) perfume ad. The scent was inspired by my travels to Bali, and the overall positioning was based on a love poem I had written.

BELOW RIGHT: My second *Interview* cover in full Balinese dress. Iris Love, the archaeologist, wrote the article. (Interview)

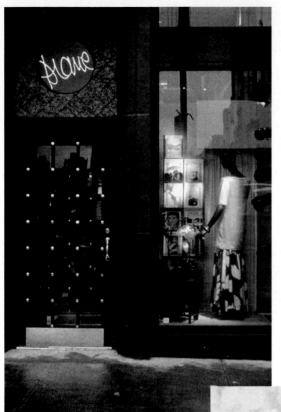

Front of my former couture boutique at the Sherry Netherland on Fifth Avenue. "A Shrine to Venus" is what I had asked the architect Michael Graves to design to house my couture collection.

Wearing the black tuxedo with a scooped back for an ad for the 1984 couture collection. Helmut Newton shot this campaign in the Plesch mansion in Beaulieu in the south of France.

(Helmut Newton)

Back to Europe with my companion, novelist
Alain Elkann. In Paris, in our Left Bank
apartment. *(Christopher Simon Sykes)*

In Egypt with Alexandre and Tatiana *(back row)*, and Alain and his children: sons John and Lapo and daughter Ginevra. We had the best time together and filled many albums with cherished memories.

ABOVE LEFT: With writer Bill Styron at Kay Graham's home on Martha's Vineyard. I see a lot of Rose and Bill Styron at home in Connecticut; Bill often comes over and watches movies with me on Saturday nights.

ABOVE RIGHT: I had admired writer Alberto Moravia all my life. When I met him and he asked me to design the costumes for one of his plays in Spoleto, I was honored. He spent long periods with Alain and me in Paris, and I gave him a great party for his eightieth birthday.
(Liorello Fabri)

I first met Nina Berberova on a plane between New York and Paris. I fell in love with this extraordinary Russian writer who had left Russia with Gorky. We became friends and I helped to publish her books in the United States. (Jean Pigozzi)

Writer Jerzy Kosinski was my friend. He often spent weekends at Cloudwalk, telling us stories and entertaining the children with magic tricks.

Screenwriter Mark Peploe with poet Fred Seidel in the "literary room" at my Paris apartment. I greatly treasure my friendships with both of them.

At the Berlin Wall with Mort Zuckerman in 1989. I shall never forget the noise of the hundreds of hammers as we watched the Wall come down.

With Dick Snyder, Mort Zuckerman, and Calvin Klein on the *Midnight Saga* to Tangier for Malcolm Forbes's birthday party in the summer of 1989.

Jane and Jann Wenner *(center)* invited Tatiana and me on a trip to the Galapagos Islands with a group that included Gil Eisner, Jean Pigozzi, Gil Friesen, Mica Ertegun, and Kate Wenner.

dated me was parents' day. The other parents always looked so much more proper and adequate than I did. I sometimes felt that they were judging me, and I couldn't wait for the day to end.

I pride myself now on the fact that I never lied to the children. We shared our lives, but we were all independent. Cloudwalk made a huge difference. There was so much room there for us all to be free and yet together. It allowed us to be close without suffocating because we all had our privacy.

I provided for my own privacy at Cloudwalk by building a bedroom in the barn (which is now adjacent to my studio) near the main house and hooking up an intercom between me and the children. Every night when I went out to my room, I would call them on the intercom to tell them that I was there and that I loved them. The nightly reassuring ritual ended abruptly when Tatiana and Alexandre were teenagers and they cut the intercom cord, literally and symbolically providing for their own privacy.

We made a lot of friends in Connecticut and saw them quite often. Bill and Rose Styron lived nearby; he the author of *Sophie's Choice*, among other powerful books, and she a social activist and at the time on the board of Amnesty International U.S.A. The designer Oscar de la Renta and his then wife, Françoise, were neighbors, as was Mike Nichols, the director of one of my favorite movies, *Carnal Knowledge*. I couldn't get enough of the Libermans, an older Russian couple whom I'd met when I first came to New York. Alexandre, the creative director at Condé Nast, and Tatiana, his extravagant, fantastic wife who had been a lover of Russian poet Mayakovsky, regaled me with great pre- and post-Revolutionary Russian stories. They had known everybody:

Picasso, Braque, Matisse, Balanchine, Sakharov. I liked them so much and envied their loving relationship. Every time I had a boyfriend in my life, I would take him to meet the Libermans. That was a test.

One summer I gave a Fourth of July picnic at Cloudwalk with everybody sitting on old quilts on the lawn. Slim Keith, another neighbor, brought the actress Claudette Colbert. Renata Adler, the writer, brought the great photographer Richard Avedon. Directors Milos Forman and Mike Nichols were there, as was the writer Jerzy Kosinski, who would describe his insomniac wanderings around the city and test our reactions on episodes I would later read in several of his books. French director Louis Malle, who had recently presented his movie *Pretty Baby* at the Cannes Film Festival, came late and there he met Candice Bergen, whom he later married.

On the one hand, I was living a fantasy life. On the other, however, I was always running behind and filled with anxiety. Though I was at the height of my success, that success was bringing ever more demands. I was flattered during a personal appearance at the Belk store in Charlotte, North Carolina, when John Belk, the mayor of Charlotte, gave me the keys to the city. A month later in New Orleans, the wife of the governor of Louisiana gave me the keys to her city. But the pressure was unrelenting. Here I was at the top, but I wasn't quite sure how I'd gotten there and, more important, where to go next. I didn't have the experience, the backup, or the structure either for me or for my company.

I had always heard that it's hard to recover from being on the cover of *Time* or *Newsweek*. So much exposure

results in such increased demand that your whole world can spiral out of control. And that is what I was beginning to sense was happening to me.

Every store that had four walls and a ceiling was stocking the dresses like there was no tomorrow. I remember in Minneapolis going to a store on one side of the street, then to another store on the other side of the street, and recognizing that both stores had all these dresses and they were all the same. "This can't go on," I remember thinking. "It doesn't make sense."

Many of my customers already had five dresses and sometimes more in their closet, and sure, they would have wanted another—but a different one. They already had a green one and a blue one. The dresses were identical. How many more could they buy?

I shared my uneasiness with my partner, Dick Conrad, but he wouldn't listen to me. Money was pouring into the company from retail sales. He was happy. The lawyer was happy, and so was the accountant. The store orders had grown so big after the *Newsweek* cover that they both decided to commit Ferretti to producing twenty-five thousand dresses a week.

I could understand their enthusiasm. The dress business was booming. But my partner wasn't in the stores. I was the one who was "schlepping" around the country to promote my clothes and launch my cosmetics line. I could see what was going on out there. The runaway growth in retail orders needed to be contained. It wasn't.

The end came abruptly. In January 1978, New York was snowed under. One incredible storm followed another, and people were skiing in the streets. But I got the biggest

chill. One dreadful Sunday morning, all the New York stores ran sale advertisements for the dresses in the newspapers. *Women's Wear Daily* followed up the next day by declaring that the market was saturated with my dresses and that the sales marked the end of a trend. The ripple effect spread through the country. The dresses went on sale from coast to coast. Orders for new dresses stopped.

I felt close to panic. Suddenly, I found myself stuck with $4 million in dead inventory. My warehouse was full of dresses, and Ferretti's factory was still pumping out twenty-five thousand new dresses a week. I stopped ordering from him, which made him very unhappy. He put intense pressure on me, but what could I do? The three little dresses I had lugged around in a suitcase just six years before had swelled to five million. Without planned growth and diversification, the collapse was probably inevitable. But it was nonetheless painful.

I felt ill advised by my partner, my lawyer, my accountant. But it was my fault, not theirs. I should have trusted my instincts and not listened to them. They, in turn, should have listened to me and taken my concerns seriously. We were all amateurs, really. We had grown so fast and become successful so fast that neither I nor the people who were involved with me were able to handle that big of a success.

The amazing thing to me was that even though the stores no longer wanted to order new dresses, the dresses were still such hot sellers on the street that I had to keep a twenty-four-hour guard in the warehouse to prevent burglaries. In 1977, the warehouse was broken into three times. Once burglars even made a hole in the roof.

Suddenly the company was on the verge of bankruptcy, but I was determined to contain the damage and preserve my reputation.

Over the next year, I restructured the company from top to bottom. I changed lawyers. I changed accountants. I bought out my partner, Dick Conrad, who had indeed made a good investment in me. Having paid $250 for a 25 percent interest in the company in 1972, he sold it back to me in 1978 for more than $1 million and made plenty in between. With a huge knot in my stomach, I determined to clean up the company and make it work. That meant unloading the dresses.

Diane Von Furstenberg dresses, after all, were still a hot property. A DVF dress license could be very lucrative, and there were a lot of people interested in acquiring the contract. The winner was Carl Rosen, a Seventh Avenue entrepreneur.

Carl was an innovator. The president of Puritan Fashions, Carl held the license on Calvin Klein jeans and had actually launched Calvin into the jeans business. It was Carl who had been behind the advertising campaign that featured a Richard Avedon photograph of Brooke Shields in the jeans over the copy line "What comes between me and my Calvins? Nothing." A huge poster of the ad hung in his office, as did memorabilia from the line he had done with Gloria Swanson called Forever Young.

Carl was a real character, a flashy, chain-smoking gambler who loved women and wore a heavy French women's perfume, Fracas. And he made me an offer I couldn't refuse: not only did he buy my entire inventory of dresses, he signed a deal with me for a minimum guarantee of $1 million a year,

plus a percentage of the royalties on dress sales to come. Once again my mother's credo had proven true: facing the worst, I had managed not only to unload a terrible liability but to work out a profitable deal.

The only problem was Angelo Ferretti. He was not pleased that I'd sold the dresses to Carl. At one point he even tried to sue me, which sent me into a panic. I received legal papers one day through lawyer Roy Cohn, Senator Joseph McCarthy's counsel during the Communist purges of the 1950s. I will never forget the terror knowing that I had Roy Cohn against me. But the suit was short lived, though for the life of me I cannot remember how I killed it. All I know is that I personally called Roy Cohn on the telephone and threatened him with something so dire that the suit was retracted. Maybe I pretended I knew something that I didn't know. I can't remember.

I managed to remain friends with Ferretti, which was important to me. For all my life, I will be thankful to him for all he did. I tried to repay him as much as I could at the time of the sale. I maneuvered a meeting between Angelo and Carl and somehow convinced the two men to work together, and for a while they did. But then Carl Rosen shifted the business to the Orient and the printed cotton knit dresses became printed silk woven dresses. The line continued to be successful for quite a while, but it was, then, a license.

I was relieved. I no longer had huge inventories. I had a new staff of professional managers to work with, including Gary Savage, whom I'd hired from Pierre Cardin fragrance to run my beauty business. A tremendous weight had been lifted off me, and I could breathe again. Since I was chairman, head designer, and now sole owner of Diane Von

Furstenberg, Ltd., the company was mine to make or break. And the signs were promising.

Just one year after I opened my beauty boutique on Madison Avenue, I received the Outstanding Personality of the Year award from the Fragrance Foundation. Instead of a liability, the dresses were flourishing as a license. So were my other licenses, including my home furnishings for Sears. Retail sales of all the products bearing my name would reach $150 million by the end of 1979 and allow me to concentrate on my growing cosmetics and fragrance business.

Newsweek had called me "the most marketable female in fashion since Coco Chanel." Now I aspired to be Estée Lauder. Having been in everybody's closet, my new goal was to be in everybody's bathroom.

THE WOMAN
I ALWAYS
WANTED TO BE

S EVENTH AVENUE WAS OVER, and Fifth Avenue began. I left the rag trade and the Garment District in 1979 without looking back and moved my offices uptown to the world of cosmetics. The new space I leased was in the old Squibb Building, the most beautiful art deco building in New York on the most prestigious corner in the world, Fifty-seventh Street and Fifth Avenue.

For my thirtieth birthday, I had given myself a beautiful sixteen-room family apartment on Fifth Avenue that had belonged to Rodman Rockefeller, Nelson's son. The apartment overlooked the reservoir in Central Park and had a view of the most beautiful sunsets—which at first the children didn't appreciate. Alexandre missed the view of the taxis he'd had from our second-floor apartment on Park Avenue, so to console him I took a picture of his old window and gave it to him.

My new offices on Fifth Avenue were at the heart of the cosmetics world. Not only did Squibb itself have a cosmetics heritage, I was just across the street from the General Motors Building, which housed the reigning king and queen of cosmetics, Revlon and Estée Lauder. The neighborhood was home to other giants as well: Bergdorf Goodman was

across the street, Tiffany & Co. was on the corner, and the Plaza Hotel was a block away.

I leased the twenty-fourth floor at 745 Fifth Avenue and designed the ten thousand square feet to look like a glamorous movie set. The floors were covered in purple carpeting except for my own office. The prior tenant had used it as a storage room, but it had a terrace, so I transformed it into my very sexy pink office.

The reception area was designed almost like a cosmetics jar, with the receptionist in the middle. The first visual as you entered the office was of pale pastel stripes of green, turquoise, and pink, including on the satin sofas. There was a huge painting of an orchid on the wall, which, in retrospect, I realize looked like an oversized vagina. I never thought it was a particularly successful painting, but the orchid became the symbol of the cosmetics line.

The big, sunny showroom faced Fifth Avenue with a view of Central Park. The rest of the office space was divided between creative services on one side, where the designers dealt with the license business, and the cosmetics business on the other. We had a laboratory in the office run by an Italian chemist named Gianni. He and his assistant worked on the different formulas for the different products, made samples, and practiced quality control. They wore white coats, as would I when I visited the lab, and it all felt very serious.

I never visited the Lauder offices, but I did visit Revlon founder Charles Revson. Revlon's offices were elegant, too, but more for the sixties and reflecting Revson's taste. My offices had a modern art deco feeling and were more of the moment. The desks had black tops, the furniture was slick. The feeling throughout was light and airy, due

partially to the building's rare luxury of having windows that could be opened. It was reminiscent of Hollywood forties glamour, like an illustration of Vargas transplanted into the eighties, and I absolutely adored it.

I was thirty-two when I moved out of the brown showroom on Seventh Avenue and Thirty-ninth Street and into the purple palace on Fifth and Fifty-seventh. The address could have been intimidating at my age, but I had a sympatico neighbor; I became great friends with Jann Wenner, the young founder and editor of *Rolling Stone* magazine, whose offices were just below mine. Jann and I jokingly called 745 Fifth the "Young Adults" building and delighted in playing tycoons. But we were both very serious about what we were doing.

Under the guidance of Gary Savage, the fragrance and cosmetics line was becoming a real business, which required a revamping of everything. Moving to Fifth Avenue was part of joining the big leagues. So was completely redesigning the packaging.

The first thing Gary Savage went after was *Tatiana*, the fragrance. We would have to do our own bottle, he decided. Our stock bottle for *Tatiana* would no longer do. Gary hired a sculptor, Serge Mansau, who had designed bottles for other perfume houses. He came up with an angled glass bottle. The image projected was that the bottle contained a multifaceted perfume for the multifaceted modern woman. But we still needed positioning. *Tatiana* is a perfume "for a woman to love and a man to remember," I explained while walking up Central Park West with Gary. *Tatiana* would be identified by that line for years, and by 1980 had become the fifth best-selling scent in the country.

We revamped the image and packaging for the cosmetics line as well. Cosmetics to me was about a perception of Hollywood glamour and old movie stars, so I gave a sexy picture of the actress Jane Russell to John Matthew, a talented illustrator who worked in our design studio, and asked him to reflect that mood in a modern way. He came back with a huge illustration of a woman holding a compact. The woman looked like me, and the scrolled design on the compact looked like a target. We called it a Beauty Target, and everything in the cosmetics line evolved from that image.

We developed a great new plastic for the compacts in marbleized white with pastel colors veining through it. In the new design, my signature became huge. The dramatic result was compacts that looked like mother-of-pearl and had a big gold signature on them.

I worked on the cosmetics themselves with Janet Chin, a beautiful young Chinese girl, and my new product development person who loved colors and makeup. I spent hours and nights and weekends with Janet over the years conceiving the most extraordinary color line in the world, which, very wisely, Gary made us call *The Color Authority*.

Hot Passion Pinks. Stop Traffic Reds. New Wave Metallics. The colors we developed were bright and daring but sophisticated and playful. Pink had been forgotten, and we brought it back in a big way. The same with purple. Both are bold colors that once again are perfect for today. Janet and I played with paints to come up with the colors; then she took them to the different factories that press powders or make lipsticks or mascara. The quality of our lipstick was probably the best in the industry, the perfect creamy texture. Janet insisted on the best, and she got it.

I've always held that cosmetics are secrets kept between women and their mirrors, and that's how I defined the line. I divided the colors into three different moods so that a woman could project the mood she wanted to be in. The pinks suggested a feminine, flirtatious mood. The reds were about authority and strength and are a bit aggressive. The browns were more neutral and natural for quieter moods. I thought the mood delineation was a very clever marketing concept then, and I still do.

I continued the theme by creating a glamour compact for each mood and its corresponding colors. The compacts were flat, light rectangles that held six lipsticks, three eye shadows, one powder, one powder shadow, the appropriate brushes to apply them with, and a lip gloss. We also did a full eye compact. The compacts were the hottest things I've ever seen in makeup and have yet to see again. Models loved them. Working women loved them. Women in general loved them. They looked and felt like expensive gambling chips and took up no room at all in one's bag.

I was so involved with the cosmetics that I paid little attention to developing a skin care line. Creating skin toners and moisturizers and astringents was very scientific and less compelling than beauty products at the time. I was more interested in making women look attractive and seductive than in science. And frankly, I was young and my skin was good. I didn't understand the importance of a skin care line.

Gary Savage and the chemists did, and they encouraged me to take more of an interest. In retrospect, of course, I realize they were right. Fragrance and skin care, not cosmetics, are the profitable sides of the business. You don't have to change skin care all the time. There is more loyalty in skin

care and once you have five or six established products, they go on forever. The same is true for fragrance, if you hit it right and can afford the high cost of establishing it. Very few fragrances become classics like Chanel No. 5 or Nini Ricci's L'Air du Temps, but in the huge industry that fragrance has become, that is the goal.

Makeup, on the other hand, is very capital-intensive and rarely profitable. As the line grew, we had so many SKU's, or stockkeeping units, that we had to rent a huge warehouse in New Jersey. It was worse than the dresses. We had thousands and thousands of labels, bottles, caps, and boxes, and an army of warehouse people on the payroll to keep track of them and practice quality control. The different products had to be packaged and every ingredient listed. Each color had a different label. Attending to so many details was complicated and expensive.

The cosmetics line also had to be changed a lot and often. Every season, just as in fashion, we had to come up with another color collection, another promotion, another mood. We introduced two or three new lipsticks and two or three new nail polishes under new names every three months.

We had amazing promotions for the new collections, all of which had themes. To promote a collection we called Atlantis, we dressed the models like goddesses from Greek mythology. For another, Stolen Kiss, the theme evolved from a voluptuous, pre-Raphaelite painting I had bought and the model echoed the Gothic sleeping beauty in the painting. For that one, we introduced a great new silver lipstick called X-Calibur.

The color line may not have been a moneymaker, but

it was satisfying. Everything that inspired me in my life I would mix with what I was creating. I felt artistically fulfilled as I created the new themes and the new colors with Janet every three months.

But it was *Tatiana,* the fragrance, that was making the money, and we expanded it into bath products—body scrub, body spray, hair and body shampoo, bubble bath, soap, talcum powder—the usual. We called the line *Tatiana Actives.*

I loved the bath products, mostly because I love to take baths. I am European, after all, not a devotee of the American shower. My relationship with water is like a cleansing ceremony, enhanced by bath oils or bubble bath. Getting dressed, doing my hair, making up my face are all parts of the ceremony, building up to the final punctuation mark of fragrance.

Because I enjoyed the sequential cleansing experience so much, I didn't incorporate all the fragrance elements of *Tatiana* into each bath product all at once but added one white flower at a time as it progressed. That way every phase of the bathing experience was one step closer to the final full bouquet of the fragrance.

Though I've never understood why, it was unusual to build a progression of scents into a product line. It seemed only logical to me that if every element was the same, by the time the woman got to the perfume, she wouldn't want it anymore; she would have had too much already. Perhaps that is why I sampled so many fragrance notes and combinations before choosing the formula for *Tatiana.* The fragrance ceremony was that important to me personally. It was also my business.

□

DIANE I WENT BACK on the road for the new cosmetics line, and in our new operating style the personal appearances I made all over the country were now even better orchestrated. Gary Savage had put together a real company with a real sales force, makeup artists, and "rotators," representatives in every city who visited the stores and set up displays. Everything would be in place when I arrived at the stores, and I would spend two hours or so there doing makeup before moving on.

Eyes were always the most important. How do you make them look big, bigger, biggest? Cheekbones were a close second. Women have always wanted cheekbones like Marlene Dietrich's, Audrey Hepburn's, Sophia Loren's. Such focal points of beauty have not changed since Cleopatra rimmed her eyes with kohl and the queens of Egypt rouged their cheeks. The women lining up for the personal appearances at stores in Dayton or Miami or Atlanta were no different.

There were always big crowds of women waiting for me at the DVF cosmetic counters—young, old, timid, pushy, proper. It took me about seven minutes to do each face. I wanted to do them fast so I could make up as many women as possible. The women seemed to enjoy it, and certainly I did.

A great deal of psychology went into the makeup sessions. The trick was to figure out what image and mood a woman wanted to project. If she were a housewife and I sensed she led a fairly dull life, we gave her a little pepper of bright pink. Red was the color of confidence for young

working women who wanted to look older or for women going in to ask for a raise. Some tasks, however, were less than joyful. "Make her beautiful," one woman whispered about her sad-looking daughter. "Her husband is having an affair."

I don't know why it meant so much to me to transform women through makeup, but it did. Some women had skin blemishes. Others had bad breath. But I didn't care. I used my fingers to put makeup on their faces and worked practically nose to nose with them until they looked in the mirror and smiled. It was like being a magician.

I continued the dialogue with women that Gigi Williams and I had started during our earlier tours. Like the customers, I was tired. My feet hurt, too. Hair was a particular bond. "I know just how you feel because I hate my hair, too," I would admit to a woman looking glumly into the mirror. By confessing my own vulnerabilities and insecurities, I made myself reachable and established a link.

The demand multiplied and then multiplied again. In 1980, the second year of the operation, the retail sales of the cosmetics and the fragrance, *Tatiana,* reached $40 million.

Perhaps it was the colors we developed. Perhaps it was the trust women had built up over the years in me and my products. Or perhaps it was the market research I could do during the personal appearances, where I could see for myself which products worked or didn't in application and what customers responded to. Whatever the explanation, the growth of the cosmetics line was beyond our expectations. I do believe we had the best line in the world and certainly the most innovative one.

Other cosmetics companies from Estée Lauder to Revlon would buy every new color the instant we came up with it and then copy it, which I found more flattering than irritating. We had the hottest cosmetics line around. As early as 1979, companies such as L'Oréal were making overtures to buy my beauty business. I had no intention, however, of selling it. I was having too much fun.

I discovered new talent in improbable places. After admiring the paintings a young artist was selling one day outside the door of Fiorucci, the trendy Italian store on East Fifty-ninth Street, I brought him to the office and commissioned him to do a painting for my nail polish. He is now a very respected and famous artist, Kenny Scharf.

I used new photographers for our advertising and discovered new models. My visual concept was a woman who looked like a woman and enjoyed it, acted like a woman and was confident, and a little aggressive, in her beauty. I found all of that in the famous—and ultimately tragic—Gia.

Gia was seventeen in 1977, when I first saw her at the Mudd Club, a rock-and-roll joint where Debbie Harry of Blondie used to hang out. She looked like a biker in a studded black leather jacket, cowboy boots, and no makeup. I couldn't believe how beautiful she was. She told me she had just arrived from Philadelphia and was doing a little modeling, though that wasn't really what she wanted to do. Later I met her again at Ara Gallant's house, which wasn't surprising because Ara's house was a cool meeting place for new beauties in town. There was something about Gia that attracted me to her, and we became friends, though she was always evasive and mysterious. To the best of my knowledge, I was the first to use her in an ad.

Gia seemed all right in the spring of 1979, when I hired her for an advertising campaign called "At the Eve of a Decade" to showcase all my products. The eight-page spread was going to run in *Vogue*, and I asked Chris von Wangenheim, the talented German fashion photographer, to shoot it. We laughed a lot and made beautiful pictures. Since I'd met her two years before, Gia had become a big cover girl, which wasn't surprising. She was the most beautiful woman ever, a cross between Julia Roberts and Cindy Crawford.

My first inkling that Gia was in trouble was during the summer, I think, of 1980. Calvin Klein lent me his house at the Pines on Fire Island, and I invited Gia for the weekend. She came with her friend Sandy, a perky blond makeup artist. At one point I walked into Gia's bedroom and found her sitting inside the closet on the floor. She became quite agitated when she saw me, but I didn't understand and didn't wonder why. Later I realized that she had probably been shooting heroin. I wish now I had been more sensitive and helpful.

I continued to try to be friends with Gia and to use her as a model, but she became very erratic. She would disappear for weeks at a time and then suddenly call me or appear in my office. Once she brought me a little cat toy, which I still have. Another time she asked me for $100. By then she was looking terrible and was obviously desperate. I felt very bad for her. This was a girl who could have owned the world and had been making as much as $10,000 a day the year before.

I didn't know what to say to her when she asked for the money. I didn't want to be patronizing, so I gave her the $100 and said that I'd like to help her in a better way. "Yes,

yes," she mumbled and went away. I never saw her again. Perhaps she had already contracted AIDS, which would lead to her death in 1986 at the age of twenty-six. Gia really was a tragic story, as indeed was Chris von Wangenheim. He died before she did, in a car accident in the Virgin Islands.

A lot of books have been written about Gia, and HBO did a movie that I have not seen. Evidently, I appear a lot in her diaries, something I didn't know until I was approached in 1997 by the producers of a documentary on her life for which I agreed to be interviewed. When I went to the studio, I saw Gia's mother being interviewed. I was intrigued to meet the mother, who was quite beautiful herself and reminded me of Gia. "I want to tell you something," she told me. "Not so long ago I was going through Gia's things and I found a letter addressed to you that she hadn't sent. I opened it and there was a poem she had written to you." I told her I would like very much to have that poem or a copy of it, but she said, "I don't think so." I have no idea why. I'll never know what was in Gia's poem, but I will always remember Gia.

MY OWN LIFE at the end of the decade was everything I had dreamed of and then some. My children were growing and filling my heart with joy and pride. Business was great, up to seventeen licenses, including Sears, and they were all going well. The dress license with Puritan was particularly successful. Some of the silk woven print dresses and separates would sell almost as many as the cotton jersey prints had at their peak.

I was more confident personally. My life was my

own and I was enjoying it. I began to like the way I looked and my curly hair. I was no longer a girl, I had become the sophisticated woman I wanted to be.

The company was going successfully and smoothly enough that I felt freer to travel. My daughter, Tatiana, was eight years old in 1979 when I took her on a trip to Venice. Alexandre was at camp, and it was the first time Tatiana and I had ever spent time alone together. I loved taking gondola rides, going shopping, and eating with my beautiful young daughter on the terrace at Cipriani. It made me feel like Silvana Mangano in *Death in Venice*. It was magical. We talked for hours. We stayed at the Gritti Palace in the same suite overlooking the Grand Canal that Hemingway had stayed in. I will always cherish the vision of Tatiana in her long night-gown with tears in her eyes waiting for me on the balcony of our room to return from dinner out. She was so sweet and I loved her so much as I consoled her with hugs and kisses. I didn't feel guilty, I must say; my mother had always left me alone in hotel rooms.

Brussels. London. Paris. I went back and forth from America to Europe, where I had begun to feel more like a glorified American tourist than a European. In Paris I stayed at the Plaza Athénée hotel, went shopping like an oil magnate from Texas, and bought sexy expensive silk underwear. Heads turned when I walked the avenue Montaigne with André Leon Talley, the very tall, very handsome, and very black Paris correspondent for *Women's Wear Daily*, whom I jokingly urged to pretend he was an African king. But no matter how glamorous my life, every time I went to Brussels to see my father I remembered the frustrated, insecure Belgian girl I had been. Though I was very happy to see my

father, who always welcomed me at the train station with red roses in his hand, I was always relieved to leave Brussels.

One friend of mine after another was getting married: Loulou de La Falaise to Thadée Klossowski, son of the painter Balthus; Nona Gordon, now Summers, the friend from the University of Geneva who had introduced me to Egon; Joan Buck, who is now the editor in chief of French *Vogue*. Weddings were in the air, everyone was growing up, and the party never seemed to stop.

The year before, I had gone to Monaco with Egon for the wedding of his cousin Princess Caroline, daughter of Prince Rainier and Princess Grace, to Philippe Junot. I had taken a suite at the Hôtel de Paris for the festivities and looked forward to what promised to be an exciting event. When I had been in Monaco with Egon six years before, I hadn't known anybody. I wanted to be really beautiful for the ball the night before the wedding and spent the entire day getting myself ready, having a facial, a massage, all of it. I was going to wear a pink Valentino ball gown with ruffles, and I put together a little crown of baby's breath I bought at the hotel florist to put in my hair. It gave me a kind of white aura around my face and was quite pretty. When Egon picked me up that night, I realized I had dressed up for him. We took pictures of one another to give to the children and went off to the party.

Because Egon was a close relative of Prince Rainier, we went to the family cocktail party before the ball. I'd never met Princess Grace before, and though she was very beautiful, I found her a bit cold. The young beautiful bride seemed torn, and I felt bad for her. It was clear that her parents were not happy with Philippe, who had quite a reputation as a

playboy. The castle itself was also a little disappointing and reminded me vaguely of the Cloisters, the branch of the Metropolitan Museum of Art that is devoted to medieval art. But once the party got going, it lived up to all expectations.

A lot of familiar faces were there from Geneva, Paris, and New York, and this time I felt easy and free amid this crowd, which used to daunt me and which now I was a part of. I drank so much champagne at the ball that night and laughed so much that the next morning my jaw ached. I felt partied out and left before the wedding ceremony.

IN 1979, I WAS INVITED to Japan to participate in a symposium on the future of women sponsored by the Japanese magazine *More* and the advertising agency Dentsu. I was flattered to be included among the rather eclectic spokespeople for women, the other guests being Lee Strasberg, cofounder of the Actors Studio; actress Faye Dunaway; Helen Gurley Brown, the editor of *Cosmopolitan* magazine; and Jane Pauley, coanchor of the *Today* show. We could each bring someone with us, and I invited my friend Ara Gallant. He cut quite a figure towering over the Japanese in his black clothes and black cap covered with gold charms.

I was fascinated by the Japanese culture and the ancient rituals and traditions that permeate every aspect of daily life from tableware to packaging to makeup. I was privileged during the conference to go backstage at a Kabuki theater and watch the actors dress and apply their stylized, chalk white Kabuki makeup. The makeup turned out to be not all that extraordinary and was just a lot of white caking and black eyeliner, but the dressing was just amazing with all

the layers of undergarments and the colors you never see on stage. I watched the leading actor, a sixty-year-old man, transform himself into a sixteen-year-old virgin girl.

I brought back crates of odd-shaped ceramic plates and dishes, old-fashioned rice paper stationery in different shapes, paints, inks, brushes. The Japanese make the most extraordinary makeup brushes in all sorts of thicknesses, which I used myself and would try to duplicate for my cosmetics business.

I left Japan filled with new ideas and inspirations. Nothing prepared me, however, for the inspiration I would find on the island Ara and I went to next: Bali.

The entry in my diary for October 23, 1979, says it all: "The happiest day of my life. Bali. An orgy of beauty, an explosion of the senses, of emotions, an encounter with harmony. It's too beautiful for words. What I have been looking for in people I've found here in nature, this blessed island, so rich, so giving, so unselfish, so beautiful, walking in the rice fields. I love this land."

The juxtaposition of the volcanoes and the sea, the luxuriousness of the rice fields and tropical forests, the sense of colors, the fabrics, the textures were all so exciting. I've never felt such freedom as I did in Bali. I got up at dawn to see the sun rise and lingered on the beach at Kuta to see the sun go down. Orange. Scarlet. Pink. Purple. The whole palette of colors in their boldness and subtleties in one sky. In the years to come, I would create a new group of orange lipsticks and call them Kuta Sunset. A new, rich fragrance would be named *Volcan d'Amour.*

I had Richard Gere to thank for introducing me to Bali. Richard was a rising actor at the time, and we had

become intimate. I had first met him years before at a party at my friend Sandy Gallin's in Los Angeles and found him to be shy and tender in spite of the image he tried to project of being tough and a rebel. He was passionate about the Orient. After the opening of his movie *An Officer and a Gentleman*, we started to see each other a lot and he told me about a trip he had just taken to Bali. When the trip to Japan came up, I suggested to Ara that we go there after the conference. I did not know during my first visit how much Bali would change my life. I only knew that there was no other place on earth that mirrored my own senses and emotions so well.

AT THE END of the 1970s, I was running fairly wild in New York, my life very much like the contrast in Bali between the volcanoes and the sea. During the day, I was a sensible, respectable businesswoman. In the evenings and on weekends, I was a loving, involved mother. The hours between midnight and 2 A.M. belonged to me and I used them with a vengeance.

New York was full of creative and sexual energy at the time. The divisions that had marked the Watergate years and the war in Vietnam had subsided, and many people had turned to pleasure. It would be the last party, really, but we didn't know that then. We were midway through the famous twenty years between the discovery of the birth control pill and the onset of the AIDS plague. Sociologists would categorize the time period as the "sexual revolution," and many women would see it as the ultimate liberation. Men had been enjoying casual relationships for centuries. Now women could, including me.

Studio 54 was the best pickup place in the world. There were always hundreds of fun, good-looking people around, talking and dancing among the props and amazing sets in the former CBS studio on West Fifty-fourth Street. The two young owners, Steve Rubell and Ian Schrager, created extravagant happenings there almost every night. And everybody wanted to go to the party.

From the moment it opened in 1977, there were always crowds of people in the street waiting to get in. At the door, there was Mark, the young blond man who had been trained to choose who was to be let in by Steve, who himself constantly checked the door. The selection process was a new and sometimes devastating form of elitism: either you had to be famous or you had to look good; money was not an issue. Studio 54 quickly became a legend, and invariably every party in town ended up there for the last drink.

I went there for the first time soon after it opened. The occasion was a birthday party Halston was giving in his town house for my longtime friend Bianca Jagger, whom I had known since 1968 in Paris. An exotic, magnificent girl from Nicaragua, Bianca was then being escorted around town by the actor Michael Caine. Mick Jagger later fell madly in love with this beautiful woman who looked very much like him, and they married. Their daughter, Jade, would become one of Tatiana's best friends.

Bianca was still with Mick at the time of Halston's party, which drew the usual crowd. Truman Capote was there, as were Liza Minnelli, Andy Warhol of course, and beautiful models such as Pat Cleveland and Patti Hansen, who would later marry Keith Richards, another Rolling

Stone. At some point late in the evening, we all went to the new club on West Fifty-fourth Street.

I'll never forget that night because I have so many pictures of it in my albums. Somehow a live white horse appeared in the club, and Bianca promptly mounted it and rode it around the stage. We laughed and danced and ate the huge birthday cake that had been prepared for Bianca. It was the first of many, many nights I would spend at the club.

I often went to Studio 54. Around midnight, I would put on my cowboy boots, drive myself to midtown in my Mercedes, park it in the nearby garage, and join in. I loved the feeling of walking in alone, like a cowboy walking into a saloon, feeling that I was breaking a taboo. Downstairs was the famous basement where all kinds of drugs and other questionable activities were going on, but I wasn't there for that. I would walk around, say hello to the people I knew, dance a little bit, meet new people, and then go home. Sometimes I didn't go home alone.

I was truly fond of two young boys I met at Studio 54 and saw often. David Geffen, the music wizard and the first of my friends who had already made serious money, introduced me to one of them. He was a proper college boy, L. J., who lived in New Jersey with his parents and was studying communications; the other, Billy, alias Jonathan, was a runaway from Buffalo who had lived on his own since he was thirteen. Jonathan periodically got into trouble with the law, but for all his rough edges, I found the "bad" boy very sweet. He gave me a dog, Roxanne, which I would keep at Cloudwalk for sixteen years.

Jonathan also gave me a switchblade, which I carried in my pocketbook. It was not to give me a sense of security, because all I did with it was peel apples. But I liked the idea of having it in my bag.

On the first business trip I took with the new president of my company, the knife was confiscated at La Guardia Airport. I'll never forget the horrified look on the face of this nice conservative man in a gray suit when security pulled out the knife on our way to Pittsburgh. I thought it was very funny, but he wasn't quite sure who he was dealing with.

I delighted in the side of me that acted tough and punk, though I don't know why. My favorite song at the time was "Love Stinks," by the J. Geils Band, which, in a spirit of delicious meanness, I sent to all my boyfriends. I was attracted to bad boys, including Richard Gere, but all of them only *looked* like bad boys.

There were lots of flirtations in my life at the time. Jann Wenner had all the *Rolling Stone* covers hanging in the lobby of his floor below mine at 745 Fifth Avenue, and I used to tease him about how many flings I had had with his cover subjects. "Just guess," I would tempt him. "Just guess." Seduction was very much part of my mood at the time: Diane, the Huntress.

Perhaps it was because I had many responsibilities and was working so hard that I could easily have slid into the stereotype of the tough businesswoman who never has fun. To have that other side of me was reassuring and a temporary escape.

The truth is that I had been deeply disappointed by the failure of my marriage. I believe in love and commitment, but sometimes life can present you with painful realities.

Instead of feeling sorry for myself, I was playing the games men play. And reversing traditional gender roles turned out to be fun.

One summer I took L. J., the college boy, to Maine, where I was going to visit Alexandre at camp over parents' weekend. L. J. stayed in the motel while I drove the rented station wagon to the camp to see Alexandre. There was nothing immoral about it. I just had this nice little boyfriend in the motel waiting for me.

My relationship with Barry remained strong and close. My flirtations did not threaten my bond with him because they were just that, flirtations, though I did feel guilty at times.

I love love. Being in love was and is an essential part of living and breathing, though I realize now that my relationships with men may seem very strange to others. I also realize that I am afraid of truly committing myself. I think, although I hate to admit it, that it may be a fear of rejection. I like to be needed, useful. I am often attracted to men who are reserved or slightly tormented, which is why I gravitate to writers and artists. I am very indulgent toward them, too indulgent probably. I accept everything and expect nothing. I've learned that if you expect nothing, what you get is a plus. So I've had a lot of pluses. I never question.... Is it fear of knowing something I don't want to know or is it respect of their privacy? I don't know.

I have never regretted a single relationship or even flirtation I've had. And almost all the men I've known have remained my friends. Sometimes it's hard to keep in touch after the breakup of a relationship, but I try not to break the dialogue. I've found that old boyfriends eventually are

reassuring and make the best and most loyal friends. Intimacy is very important to me.

DIANE Men would make me suffer, of course. I have felt rejected and sometimes betrayed, but I don't think you can feel love without some suffering. I'm not sure these men even knew I was suffering because I would rarely show it. I'm not confrontational, I never get into fights and I have no memory for pain. When, in my mind, the relationship is on the decline, I go away and withdraw, and usually someone else appears. And then, unfortunately, it is over. It is at that point, inevitably, that they start to miss me. In truth, the men I've loved and cared for have never treated me as well during the relationship as they have after.

I had occasional yearnings to be taken care of and to give up my independence, but the moments passed. I was seeing too many of my friends give up their own identities to please their husbands or lovers, only to be lost when the relationships ended. A steady stream of angry, confused friends from Brussels, from school, from the University of Geneva were coming to New York or to Cloudwalk to stay with me while they tried to figure out who they used to be and what to do with their lives. By comparison, my life was my own and I cherished it.

"TODAY I'M THIRTY-THREE," I wrote in my diary on the eve of January 1, 1980. "During this last decade, I've changed so much and learned so much, it seems crazy—almost impossible. Now a new period. A new page. In the ten years to follow, I will be able to enjoy the seeds I planted during the '70s."

I didn't know that three months later, my life would take a completely unexpected turn.

I had never thought deeply about being Jewish. God is inside me and nature is more of a comfort and inspiration to me than organized religion. I knew about my mother's near death in the Nazi concentration camps. But she had always put such a determinedly positive face on the horror that I had accepted her version of the story. I was wrong.

The sequence of events began in April 1980 at a country inn in Germany, where my mother had gone with her Swiss companion, Hans, on a business trip. One evening they were dining with a group of Germans at a big table where the conversation was loud and boisterous. That night Hans woke up to find that my mother was not in their bedroom. He looked for her, called for her, but she seemed to have vanished. He alerted the hotel staff, who joined the search. They found her hiding under the concierge desk in the lobby, unable to speak.

I didn't understand what Hans was telling me when he called from Germany to say that my mother was very ill and that he was driving her home to Geneva, and that I should come as soon as possible. I began to understand when I tried to talk to her. Her mind was off somewhere else. She was laughing, crying, babbling incoherently. When I got to Switzerland the next day, and I saw her in the hospital, she looked like a shrunken bird in the big fur coat she didn't want to relinquish. She would be staying in the mental ward for the next three weeks.

Sometimes she knew me, sometimes she didn't. When she spoke, her voice was loud and her speech slurred, as if she were drunk. I stayed with her in the hospital, and for

the first time, I began to understand about the camps. The pain and the memories she had hidden from us and from herself for thirty-five years seemed to be breaking free, but in disconnected bits and pieces. Listening to her was like listening to a broken tape recording because most of what she said was incoherent.

In the hospital I thought at times that I was the one who was going mad. My mother's ravings and the screams of the other mental patients overwhelmed me until I couldn't be sure that I was not screaming, too. I was unable to sleep, and when I did, exhausted, I had nightmares in which I became my mother. I was so upset that I lost my passport and then could barely cope with the bureaucratic red tape of securing a new one. Only the needs of the children, whom I'd brought to Geneva from Italy, where they were visiting their other grandmother, kept me sane. I bought them roller skates and hired someone at the hotel to look after them.

My father came from Brussels. My brother came as well. We were helpless in the face of the agony my mother was reliving. She wouldn't eat. She wouldn't drink. We worried that she was on her way back down to the forty-nine pounds she'd weighed when she was liberated. "I want to win this battle against those evil demons," I wrote to my mother in my diary. "I promise I will avenge you of all these horrors and get you out of there. I swear it."

In the end my mother healed herself. It was as if she said to herself, "I'll either die here or get out of here." And she began to recover. She was very confused about where she was and why she was in the hospital, as were we. No one ever really found out what had happened to her on that night in

Germany. But she was a miracle once again, coming back to life from far away.

I thought I had known her so well, but I hadn't. Though she was one of the lucky ones who had escaped death in the camps, obviously she hadn't escaped totally. My mother and the millions of others who had suffered remained prisoners of the atrocities they had endured. The Nazis had wanted them to be naked and servile, and to some extent they still were. They would not forget the nightmare of the camps. Nor would I—nor should I.

I hadn't wanted to face the unthinkable of what had happened during the Holocaust and certainly not what had happened to my own mother. Like many others, I had blanked it out as too awful to contemplate. Even after my mother's breakdown, I continued to keep the truth at arm's length. It was impossible to absorb.

It would be another year before I confronted it again. The occasion was a luncheon given in New York by the Anti-Defamation League of B'nai B'rith at which I was to receive a Woman of Achievement award. I was honored, but I'd just returned from a trip to Bali and my head was elsewhere. "Do I have to go to the lunch?" I asked my secretary.

"Of course you do," she said. So I went.

As I sat there listening to the speeches about discrimination and injustice, I became more engaged. When I went up on the dais to receive my award, I surprised myself and everyone else by saying what I had never said and never faced. "Many of you know me because you wear my dresses," I told the thousand women in the audience. "What very few people

know is that eighteen months before I was born, my mother was in Auschwitz."

A gasp ran through the audience. There were tears in people's eyes, as there were, suddenly, in mine. I found myself trembling, shaking. Unable to finish my remarks, I rushed out. I was stunned at the vulnerability I had never even known I had. But that day turned out to be a turning point. As a child of a survivor, I realized it was very important for me to talk about the Holocaust. It became one of my life causes, and I would involve myself with the National Holocaust Museum in Washington, D.C., by speaking there on occasion and helping the museum to raise money.

My MOTHER'S BREAKDOWN caused me to examine other areas of my life and to reorder my priorities. I was filled with so many heavy emotions when I left Geneva while my mother was recuperating in a clinic that I knew I had to get as far away from everything as possible. I returned to New York, packed three bags, took a child by each hand, and flew to Bali.

I walked the beach for miles at sunrise and sunset and kept in daily contact with the office by telex. The children and I traveled the island to find textiles, carvings, and old doors, which I shipped home to Cloudwalk. We climbed the volcanoes and dressed like the islanders in colorful sarongs we bought on a side trip to Java. Tatiana and I wore frangipani in our hair, and we all ate delicious food flavored with the spices we had bought at the Denpasar spice market.

The simple pleasures of Bali were a contrast to the hectic life I had left behind in New York. The allure of the

bad boys, including Richard Gere, faded. At the time, Richard, ironically, was appearing in *Bent,* a play about the Holocaust, in New York. My infatuation for Richard had grown and I had become obsessed with him. I didn't like the feeling. I exorcised him from my life altogether at five o'clock one morning while walking on the beach. "Forget Richard," I wrote in large letters in the sand. On the way back along the beach, I met Paulo. Paulo Fernandes was Brazilian, his curly beard smelled like cloves, and he wore a sarong with great elegance.

Far from my pressured world in New York, Paulo represented calm and serenity. He didn't seem to care about business or social status. He was an unassuming designer and a connoisseur and dealer of primitive art who lived simply in a bamboo beach house and hadn't worn shoes in ten years. I fell in love with him and would remain faithful to him for the next four and a half years.

The relationship was not always easy. Paulo soon decided to transfer himself to New York, but the transition to my Fifth Avenue apartment with its leopard-print carpeting and all my famous friends was a lot for him to absorb. He had little in common with my New York life. For me, he represented a new life and brought out a part of me that wanted to be more submissive to a man, that wanted to have a more domestic life.

Barry and I stopped living together when Paulo entered my life. Our relationship would survive, however. Barry made the adjustment from lover to friend. His love would turn out to be the deepest of all.

Change followed change. For some time I had been uneasy about the children's lives in New York. They were ten

and eleven in 1981, old enough to travel back and forth on their own to school and to visit their friends and therefore old enough to be in danger I thought. Calvin Klein's teenage daughter, Marci, had been kidnapped in the street in 1978 and held briefly for ransom. Though she had been released unharmed, the incident had frightened me.

I also didn't like the pseudosophisticated life many New York children led. Many of them were too hip, too jaded, too out of touch with nature. Every day was super-managed with one activity after another, leaving them no time simply to be. I wanted my children to develop their imaginations and their personalities by entertaining themselves instead of always being entertained. In a curious return to the childhood I'd hated in Brussels, I saw the advantages of a little boredom. And so I abruptly changed their lives.

Tatiana would take years to forgive me, but in 1981 I took the children out of New York and moved us all to Cloudwalk full time. I enrolled them into the nearby private school, Rumsey Hall. Alexandre loved the freedom of the country and began his lifelong love affair with engines—snowbikes, motorbikes, anything that went *rummm rummm.* The space of the grounds and the vastness of the sky allowed him to use his imagination the way he never could in New York. He was sure, and deep down still is, that a UFO was going to land on the lawn. Tatiana fought the move to Connecticut until she made a new best friend at school, Beata, who spent so much time at our house that after a few months her mother let her come and live with us.

I made over my own life as well. Cloudwalk became my base instead of the apartment on Fifth Avenue. I lived in Connecticut with Paulo and the children during the week

and commuted to New York. My social life was minimal, and to my surprise, I liked that. But I also enjoyed getting into my car in the morning, driving to New York, and leading a man's life again. I needed the balance.

Cloudwalk came to life as a center for the children's friends. I've always believed that children deserve their freedom as much as adults do. That freedom would get somewhat out of hand during the children's teens, when Cloudwalk would briefly turn into a disgusting party house. We all lived through it, however. It gives me great pleasure now when those same children, now grown and married, bring their own children to Cloudwalk.

FOR MANY, Cloudwalk was a home away from home, though with fewer rules. I didn't mind the mess the children and their friends made in the house, the dirt they tracked in, the games that were strewn all about. It was more important to me to know where my children were and to know their friends.

The projection room Barry had given us was a great draw. So were the colorful ceremonial flags along the river that I had brought back from my first trip to Bali. The twenty-foot-high flags in bright red and yellow and blue and green looked so beautiful and seemed such a celebration of life to me. I still have the flags; we keep changing them as they weather. My dear friend Hugo, another Brazilian who lives in Bali, sends me new ones every year.

Bali and all things Indonesian ran through my new designs. The colors of the sky over Kuta beach inspired my new Sunset Goddess line of cosmetics. The richness of the

archipelago's textiles and batiks covered the furniture and walls in my office and found their way not only into my designs but into all facets of my life. For four years, I only wore sarongs.

My mother thought I was crazy. "Why don't you wear real clothes?" she would ask me. But I loved them. In the winter I wore woven ikats with boots and sweaters; in the summer, I wore cotton batiks with T-shirts and sandals. By 1981, Bali and Paulo's bamboo house near the beach had become my spiritual home, and the sarongs served as a reminder of that link.

I was having fun being in love with Paulo and Bali while developing a new fragrance with the temporary code name "Deadly Feminine." With little thought of cost, I commissioned Dakota Jackson, a friend and furniture designer, to create a bottle for the new scent and Antonio Peticov, another Brazilian friend and artist, to design the box to house it.

We needed a marketing position for the new fragrance, and in a meeting with Gary Savage I suggested that the positioning be love. I then produced a copy of a love note I had written to Paulo during a plane flight to Chicago when he was in one section of the plane and I in another:

> *Into my life you came*
> *Bringing peace to my heart*
> *Fire to my body*
> *Love to my soul*
> *In your eyes I see myself*
> *Feeling, reaching, looking*
> *For perfect harmony.*

Though the poem hadn't been written as a marketing strategy, it became one. We decided to name the new scent *Volcan d'Amour* (Volcano of Love), which I dedicated to Paulo, and to include the love note in the packaging. From inception to launch, *Volcan d'Amour* incorporated every aspect of my sense of design and personality at the time.

For the announcement of *Volcan d'Amour* at a press breakfast in my office in 1981, I flew in thousands of frangipani from Hawaii and arranged them in pyramids to evoke the Balinese volcanoes. We served apricot pancakes and played gamelan music. At the launch of the fragrance at Saks later that day, I dressed the models in blue sarongs I had designed and had them hand-painted with gold volcanoes at the Denpasar market.

I was getting increasingly nervous, however. On the one hand, the company was doing extremely well. We had come from near bankruptcy in 1977 to gross sales of all products in 1981 of $245 million. On the other hand, I was worried that the cosmetics line was growing too rapidly. The knot in my stomach that had been caused by the panic of failure in 1977 was being tightened again in 1982 by the panic of success. More and more department stores wanted to carry the cosmetics, which meant that more and more money had to be spent on advertising, promotion, and display. The little cosmetics shop on Madison Avenue was long gone.

The demand for the cosmetics and scents also meant having to keep greater and greater amounts of inventory. The reality of having to buy and stockpile millions of dollars' worth of bottles and tops terrified me. I began to have nightmares about warehouses filled with my beauty products, just as they had been with the dresses. I had nightmares about

meeting the payroll. By 1981, the company staff had grown to well over three hundred and the payroll was $1 million a month.

The licenses were bringing in a lot of income, which we used to finance the cosmetics and perfume line. But the cost of launching *Volcan d'Amour* promised to be enormous. Gary Savage kept on building sales, while Sheppard Zinovoy, the company president I had terrorized with the switchblade at La Guardia Airport, kept on borrowing money from Chemical Bank to cover our operating expenses.

The overextension of our financial position lay in the computer printouts Gary and Shep gave me every week. But I never opened the kilos and kilos of those huge, heavy reports they gave me. I had no interest in trying to understand them. It was their job, after all, to protect the company financially. My job was to have the ideas, create the products, make sure they were desirable, and go out and sell them.

There is no doubt that I was somewhat distracted at the time. I have always been seduced by men who are good travelers, and I was away quite a lot, traveling with Paulo to remote and exotic islands in Indonesia looking for rare statues and textiles. I was paying much less attention to the business side of the business and much more to the fun of creativity. While the company president was borrowing money in New York, I was in Bali working with painters on the promotional materials for *Volcan d'Amour* for department store counters. I was not thinking about how much money would be needed for the launch.

I was in Paris in 1982 when the call came in from my office in New York. Chemical Bank was refusing to release any more money to the company unless I signed a personal

note of guarantee. A personal note? Suddenly all I saw was loss—the loss of Cloudwalk, the loss of my apartment. There was no way I could do that.

I returned from Paris to meet with the banker at Chemical and was stunned to discover that I owed it $10 million. Oh my God! I thought, How could I owe so much money? "What do you want me to do?" I asked the banker. "Sell the company?" I'll never forget the condescending expression on his face. "If you can," he scoffed. Then I got mad.

Numerous companies had approached me over the years about buying my business. At times I had been tempted. Waiting for a plane at Pittsburgh airport in 1980, I had written in my journal, "I'm tired. I'm fed up. What am I doing? Who knows? I don't want to be stuck. God, I don't want to be stuck." Three years later, my hand was being forced. I decided to take charge.

Gary and I quietly began negotiations with Beecham, a big English pharmaceuticals company, which was in the process of creating a cosmetics division. I didn't tell anyone else in the company about it, including the new financial officer. By then, the president of my company had left by mutual consent.

Beecham's first official offer came in on March 12, 1983: $20 million plus 3 percent royalties on sales for twenty-five years and an annual consulting fee of $100,000. Gary and I met with our lawyers, who agreed that we could do better, and ten days later we all flew to London to continue negotiations. I was playing in a very-high-stakes game, and we did very well. Beecham raised its offer to $22 million, sweetened the royalties a bit, and kept the same consultant's fee. We

accepted. But there was a hitch: Beecham's board of directors had to be consulted, and the deal could not be finalized before June at the earliest and probably July.

The three-month hiatus was a nightmare. Chemical Bank was pressuring me for money to repay the loans. The financial officer of my company was pressuring me for money to pay the employees. "We won't be able to make payroll next month," he kept telling me. I was a wreck. But I still didn't tell anyone about the pending sale, even at the companywide sales meeting in Boca Raton. I was superstitious enough not to want to jinx anything, and, more important, I didn't want to create a panic among the staff.

The deal with Beecham Cosmetics was finally signed on July 13, 1983. I had managed to sell the company with great glory, even though it had been at the eleventh hour. "Celebration," I wrote in my diary. "I feel free, rich and relieved." The smug little banker at Chemical got his $10 million, and I was $12 million ahead.

Still, a part of me was quite disappointed. For years and years I had hidden behind men in suits whom I had trusted to run my companies. But the men had not lived up to expectations. The first suit had left me with too many dresses in 1978. The second suit had run up so much debt that I had had to sell the cosmetics business at the very last minute. Though I had a fantastic product line, wonderful real estate in my counter positioning in the department stores, and an untarnished reputation, the business position I was in was pathetic. But it wasn't as much the fault of the men in suits as my own. I had not paid attention to the reality of the business.

On the other hand, I relished my new freedom. For

the first time in ten years, I didn't have the pressures of owning and running a company, of maintaining stockrooms and warehouses, of feeling responsible for so many employees, including Gary, who would go to work for Beecham. By achieving so much at thirty-six, I could enjoy the luxury of early retirement. I had come out of it a rich woman.

Cloudwalk was secure. My apartment was secure. My children were secure. And so was I. In the thirteen years since I'd arrived in America with a dream and twelve dresses in a suitcase, I'd created and sold two companies. My signature was worth millions of dollars to the companies who licensed my products. Yet it bothered me that for the first time in more than a decade, I no longer had control over my own name.

THE OTHER WOMAN IN ME

I LOVE TO BUY my own jewelry, and I like it to mean something special. If I break up with a man, for example, I will buy a ring. The ring stands for a commitment to myself; it's really no different from its traditional role as a symbol for commitment to another. Whenever I need an icon to mark a beginning or a turning point, I buy myself a piece of jewelry.

Which is why, soon after the sale to Beecham, I went to A la Vieille Russie, the prestigious antiques store in the Sherry Netherland Hotel on Fifth Avenue in New York, and bought an eighteenth-century English parure. The exquisite Victorian set of large aquamarine brooch, necklace, and earrings celebrated the sale and was a gesture of appreciation from me to myself.

On the other side of the hotel lobby I spotted an attractive empty space. Because all the products that now carried my name were controlled by third parties, I was looking for a window, somewhere, through which I could totally create and control an image for my brand name.

The store had once been a pharmacy and, more recently, a men's shop. I felt its location would fit the eighties fashion scene. The Jimmy Carters' cloth coat culture was definitely over, and Nancy Reagan's fur coat era had arrived. Where material concerns had been considered a vice in the

1960s and 1970s, money and greed were fast becoming signs of virtue, as demonstrated by the huge audience that sat glued to the television set every Wednesday night to watch *Dynasty*.

Why wouldn't a beautiful shop in the Sherry Netherland be the perfect stage for a new couture collection of beautiful made-to-order dresses I would design for the decade's more affluent, showier woman? I envisioned the upscale accessories the customers of the eighties would be able to buy in the shop, along with the treasures I would collect in my world travels. The shop at 783 Fifth Avenue would reflect the new aura of sumptuousness and extravagance. Without thinking left or right, I leased the store and embarked on this new adventure.

I hired Michael Graves, the world-renowned architect, to design his first retail store, which I planned to name: Diane. "Make it a little shrine to Venus," I told Michael. "Make it a place where a woman can walk in and dream and fantasize and for a man who wants to indulge her." Two million dollars later I would have just that shrine, a two-story boutique with a gold-leafed Grecian vessel designed by Michael in the glass over the front door (to "gather in light and symbolize the feminine spirits"), a double-height oak-floored entryway, a tented salesroom on the first floor, trompe-l'oeil marble and faux copper latticework on the stair wall, and pink carpeting throughout the second floor's couture presentation and dressing rooms.

To help design the collection, I brought my friend Stephan Janson, a young, talented French designer who had worked with me previously, back from Italy. We chose the most beautiful and precious fabrics—silks and cashmeres from Italy, intricate laces from France, rich wools from Ire-

land. Though the clothes were a major departure from the affordable fashion I had always insisted on in the past, the first indications were very promising. We would have $75,000 in orders before the store opened in the winter of 1984. Aretha Franklin bought a ball gown of pink silk and black lace over the phone for $3,500, and so did a woman in Houston who had seen the gown in an ad. Brooke Shields bought a black tuxedo, and Bianca Jagger bought silk evening pajamas.

The ads for the collection were very dramatic, I thought. Helmut Newton, the famous German photographer known for his erotic images of women, shot incredibly intense photos of me for the launch at the Plesch mansion in Beaulieu in the south of France. I had always dreamed of being photographed by Helmut and being one of the powerful women he captures with his lens. And I was that in his pictures, modeling our new ball gowns from Diane and in a black tuxedo with a veil over my eyes. The pictures, the clothes, the shop, all of it was a strong statement.

Couture clothes have always been the tip of the retail pyramid, and they are created by just such images. The image had to project the message: it's fashion, it's elegance, it's expensive, it's a new Diane. I hoped it would also help the licenses.

I ran the advertisements for Diane in a very early issue of *Vanity Fair.* Everybody told me I was crazy to invest in a magazine they felt sure wouldn't last, but I had met and liked Tina Brown, the clever British editor who had taken it over. I had invited her to lunch soon after she had arrived from England to welcome her to New York and to pick her brain about finding an English boarding school for my

daughter Tatiana. I also ran the ads for Diane in *W, Town & Country*, and *Connoisseur*, and I was right about *Vanity Fair*. The magazine's image proved to be upscale but edgy and just like the clothes.

Shopping for the store, I went to Scotland for the first time in 1984 with Stephan, my friend Olivier, who would be running the store, and Paulo, who was involved in the business by then. Though it wasn't the season for gorse and heather, it was, as ever, the season for cashmere. We went from one cashmere factory to another along the Tweed River, buying scarves and sweaters. I had never visited Scotland and I loved it. The great diversity of tartans according to clans reminded me of the variety of Indonesian ikats.

I had a whole new set of clothes to wear and promote that were a far departure from the little jersey knits and the easy printed silk dresses. I wore the black tuxedo to Gloria Steinem's fiftieth birthday party at the Waldorf-Astoria and it got a lot of attention. The back of the tuxedo was slightly scooped and décolleté, so I wore my hair up and finished off the look with a net over my eyes topped by a single red rose. It was a great party. Gloria had gathered hundreds of friends and women supporters. She looked radiant. I remember thinking how great it would be to look that way at fifty and have accomplished that much. Gloria had given "a key to freedom" to many women and I had always admired her.

I was going through a personal passage of my own at the time, and the new clothes were indicative of that. No more simple sarongs. I was restless in my life at Cloudwalk with Paulo, and he was restless, too. There were tensions all

around. Neither of the children was getting along particularly well with Paulo. And they were acting like the teenagers they had become. Alexandre got his driver's license and within a week had his first accident. Tatiana was in a car accident as well, though she wasn't driving. Cloudwalk had become a party house of sorts, which I didn't like at all. It was time for the children to go to boarding school, and I spent a lot of time touring schools in New England with Alexandre and in England with Tatiana. Her friend Jade Jagger was also planning to go to boarding school in England, and I remember fondly spending a whole afternoon with her father, Mick, in his kitchen on the Upper West Side looking through the prospectuses of English schools. Mick, the son of schoolteachers, took the process very seriously.

All these changes were occurring at the same time I was developing the store and the couture line. I felt distracted. Barry, too, was at a turning point. I was visiting him in Los Angeles for the 1984 Summer Olympics when he told me he was contemplating leaving Paramount. He had brought a little typewriter from his office, and together we wrote his letter of resignation. Everybody around me seemed poised on the brink of a new life, and I was increasingly eager for one of my own.

I was attracted by the dramatic changes going on in Europe. The promise of a unified Europe by 1992 was an exhilarating idea to me. I bought blue European Union flags with twelve stars on them and stuck stickers all over my bathroom. Modern Europe was being led by intellectuals, many of them socialists, which also appealed to me. François Mitterrand was president of France. Felipe González, my activist friend from the University of Madrid, was prime

minister of Spain, and Bettino Craxi was premier of Italy. Their administrations would all end up in corruption of some sort, but in 1984 I didn't know any of that. I only knew that in the middle of launching a new venture in America, I was yearning for Europe.

It all began to come clear in the summer of 1984, when I chartered a sailboat to cruise the Greek islands. The cruise with Paulo, my children, and Hugo, the Brazilian friend of the family I invited along to diffuse the tension between Paulo and the children, should have been a reward, but it wasn't. My children had always welcomed my friends as I had theirs. They were so clearly the number-one priority in my life that they had never felt threatened by my affections. They would, however, get defensive when they believed I was being taken advantage of. It wasn't really the case with Paulo, but for some reason, they had stopped trusting him. The atmosphere on the boat was very tense. I knew, lying on the deck in the sun, that I had come to the end of a cycle and that my life would change.

In the fall, I delivered Tatiana to the English boarding school she'd chosen in an old castle in Wiltshire surrounded by an amazing garden designed by Capability Brown, one of the most famous landscape architects of all time. I cried nonstop the whole way home from England to New York. Tatiana would spend one year there before going on to school in Switzerland. Alexandre went off too, but to board for a year at the school near Cloudwalk where he'd been a day student. He too, would go on to another boarding school the following year. Then I went to the hairdresser in New York and had my hair chopped off.

There is no clearer sign to a woman that she is willing for a new life to emerge. And it did.

I MET ALAIN ELKANN in October 1984 at the thirteenth birthday party Bianca Jagger gave for her daughter, Jade. The attraction was immediate and not at all that surprising to me. The night before the party, I was sitting in the kitchen with Paulo and Jerry Brown, who had mysteriously reappeared, when I suddenly thought, something new and major is going to happen in my life. The very next night I went to Bianca's party by myself and met Alain.

Alain was a very attractive Italian writer who lived in Paris. Slim and impeccably dressed, he had beautiful blue eyes and an angular face. His marriage had just broken up when I met him, and he seemed desperate and very needy, qualities I have always found irresistible in men.

Alain and I had many tastes, friendships, and even relatives in common. He had married Gianni Agnelli's daughter, and I had married Clara Agnelli's son, which made Alain's three children and mine second cousins. And like me, he was Jewish. Without further thought I threw myself into this new relationship. We talked all night and I did not get home until the next morning. I would remain faithful to Alain for the next five years.

My new transatlantic relationship complicated the new couture business. I went back and forth to Paris all the time after I met Alain. In the winter of 1984, I made a quick trip from Paris to New York to open the store, but my heart was not in it and I immediately returned to France. The

future of my couture line was obviously threatened, but at the time I didn't really care. Besides, designing very expensive products that only a few can afford was definitely not something I truly enjoyed.

Alain's world was ideas and books and European identity, which had been my own as well. He was also very lost at a time I wanted to be needed. My children were away at boarding schools, and my new business didn't really mesh with the new life I craved. My licensing business was frustrating. The licenses, in fact, were beginning to lose momentum.

The disintegration had begun slowly after I had sold the beauty business in 1983. The licensees were looking at the competition and copying other designs rather than listening to my recommendations. The products were becoming average, and the licensees were finding it harder to get their products into the top-rank stores. The dress license was also beginning to founder because it compromised the integrity of the brand for the sake of more volume.

The distribution of the licensed products began to change, and for the worse. Because I had been so naive when I originally signed many of the contracts, I hadn't specified or restricted the distribution of the products. The licensees felt free to sell my name in any market, including high-volume discount stores. While my income from the royalties was still going up, my name was on a slow downward retail spiral, which was yet another incentive for me to start a new life in Europe.

I sold the Fifth Avenue apartment in 1985. It was overcrowded with things and more things from the life I had already begun to leave in 1980 by moving to Cloudwalk with Paulo and the children and continued to distance myself

from by moving to Paris with Alain. Though I had certainly enjoyed the powerful, hard side of me that acted like a man, the other woman in me wanted to be vulnerable and feminine. Since 1980, it had become more important to me to be the faithful woman of a man than to be a businesswoman on her own with five phone lines.

I had begun to boil down my identity with Paulo so it wouldn't threaten his own. I went further, much further, to accommodate my relationship with Alain. I didn't realize that, in the end, I would come close to losing my identity altogether.

THERE HAS ALWAYS BEEN a side of me that likes to think I would do anything for love. The idea of the characters Anna Karenina and Emma Bovary is appealing to me, and I lived it to its fullest in Paris. Alain hated my edgy clothes, so I reshaped my image. I gave up my spike heels and wore the flat shoes he gave me, and traded in my avant-garde tuxedo for tweed skirts and sweaters. My new bookish image was very much in contrast to the glamorous image of me in the Helmut Newton ads that were simultaneously running in the magazines, and the contradictions eventually made me a bit schizophrenic.

My new, private image made my children smile. They had long teased me about having no personality of my own because I changed it so often. They had watched me go from wearing only Balinese sarongs with Paulo to looking like a schoolteacher with Alain. They claimed I changed my personality for whatever man I was with and was no more than a boring doormat. But I thought my different manifesta-

tions, including my new life in Paris, were simply different parts of me. Not only did I want the relationship with Alain to work, I wanted and needed a change.

Alain was an established novelist. At the time I met him, he had just finished a novel called *Piazza Carignano.* It is the story of an uncle of his who had been a strong supporter of the fascist movement in Italy even though he was a Jew. I found the book fascinating and Alain irresistible. I plunged into the new role of writer's companion with delight. I did spend hours on the phone to my office and returned to New York almost once a month, but I lived his life.

Alain needed a lot of attention, and I was glad to give it to him. I became a writer's muse and companion, and I enjoyed it. I would listen to him read what he'd written and do all the devoted things one does when one lives with a writer. I accepted the agony of the creative process and perfected being quiet and not making demands. Where he went, I went.

Alain was also the representative in Paris for Mondadori, the biggest Italian publishing house, and I accompanied him on his frequent trips to Italy and to all the book fairs— in Frankfurt, in Turin, in Jerusalem. We traveled to Argentina and Brazil, where I met my favorite writer and author of *Kiss of the Spider Woman*, Manuel Puig, who became a friend. I also met Ernesto Sábato, whose book *The Tunnel* I had read as a teenager, and Buoy Casares, who had been a great friend of Jorge Luis Borges. We traveled to Israel, where we met Aharon Appelfeld, whose work would be launched in America by Philip Roth and who would visit me at Cloudwalk. Life was interesting, pleasant, and easy, and I made myself as helpful as I could, organizing the house, the trips, and most

of all by being available. I was very much in love and tried to please him more than I had ever done before. I also got very close to his children, John, Lapo, and Ginevra.

I decorated a beautiful apartment on the rue de Seine on the Left Bank that I still have. I did an extensive renovation, restoring the wood floors, which dated from the French Revolution, and furnishing the apartment with the European, not Balinese, antiques from my New York apartment. Everything that was Balinese was forbidden by Alain. It couldn't even be in the vocabulary.

I designed the apartment as Bohemia Luxuria, because I had long since discovered that writers may act bohemian, but they love luxury. The apartment runs like a bridge between the courtyard and a private garden and has beautiful proportions. The very high ceilings were perfect for the huge Orientalist and pre-Raphaelite paintings of women I had bought at Sotheby's in New York for very little in the 1970s, when no one had been buying them, and which had become quite fashionable. I divided the collection between the new, smaller apartment I was renting in New York and the apartment in Paris.

I loved rediscovering the city I had lived in at twenty. From the apartment I could walk across the Seine to the Right Bank and be right at the Louvre. On the Left Bank, it is near the École des Beaux-Arts and the Académie-Française. The apartment fulfilled yet another fantasy: ever since my school days, I had dreamed of creating a literary salon in the tradition of Bloomsbury, Simone de Beauvoir, and Colette. The writers and artists who visited us, and often stayed with us, made it seem a reality.

Alberto Moravia, the most influential Italian novelist

of the century, lived with us for almost two years. Alain was writing a biography of Moravia, and getting to know Alberto so intimately was an extraordinary experience. I had worshiped his books as a young girl. Alberto was very handsome, his sharp eyes did not need reading glasses, and he had the most expressive hands I ever saw. He had a very young and beautiful Spanish wife, Carmen. Their relationship was passionate and full of confrontations. He loved staying with us on the rue de Seine, and we loved having him. When Alberto asked me to design the costumes for one of his plays that was being produced in Spoleto, I was incredibly flattered.

Our apartment was a center for other writers because of Alain's association with Mondadori and the many writers we had as friends. Many of those friends would stay with us in what I called the Literary Room.

The apartment was big enough to transform itself to accommodate whoever was there. Sometimes it was just Alain and me with a writer in one of the extra bedrooms. On weekends, the apartment could accommodate Alain's three children, or, when my children were there, all five children. There was no formal dining room but different corners where we could set up tables. The concept was one of an ongoing, moving stage, which fit very much with how I saw my life then.

Writers loved to stay in the apartment and continue to do so. The apartment is very quiet, and Paris is inspiring. The Latin Quarter is an artist's neighborhood and filled with cafés. Picasso lived there. Oscar Wilde lived and died four houses away from the apartment, and the Café Flore, the café frequented by Jean-Paul Sartre, is just two blocks away. Ni-

cole Wisniak, the red-haired, ethereal-looking founder of the most luxurious magazine in the world, *L'Égoïste,* lived above us. Whether it is the air, the wine, or the ambiance, somehow it is easier for writers to write in Paris.

Mark Peploe, who wrote the screenplay for the movie *The Last Emperor,* wrote a lot of the screenplay for *The Sheltering Sky* in the apartment. Bret Easton Ellis, the author of *American Psycho,* spent around two months in the apartment, as did James Fox, the author of *White Mischief,* who was working on a new book. The Italian writers Enzo Siciliano and Pier Vittorio Tondeli stayed with us, as did the American poet Fred Seidel, who finished his book *My Tokyo* in the apartment.

They were all part of the literary mix in Paris and the rich cultural life that I craved after my reclusive years at Cloudwalk. I was hungry for the exchange of ideas, a side of me that I had neglected, and I was pleased beyond measure to be back into it. I gave Alberto Moravia his eightieth birthday party in the apartment, and we entertained painters, writers, editors, politicians, architects, and actors such as Marcello Mastroianni and Anouk Aimée.

It was at one of these parties in 1986 that I decided to help Gérard-Julien Salvy start a publishing company. Gérard-Julien, who had introduced the work of Paul Bowles, author of *The Sheltering Sky,* and Bruce Chatwin, the author of *In Patagonia* and *The Songlines,* in France was interested in publishing other well-known authors in France.

Salvy Publishing was the fulfillment of one more dream. We used good paper and design, and our books were as beautiful as the contents. We translated published British writers such as Vita Sackville-West, Cyril Connolly, and

Barbara Pym, and Gregor von Rezzori. I was thrilled when Moravia gave me two of his short stories to publish.

For all that my life in Paris was very fulfilling and interesting, Alain was extremely difficult and possessive. He didn't want me to have any life separate from his, which, for the most part, was all right with me. Our interests were very similar. But at times, his possessiveness—and my acquiescence—would lead to events I regret.

In 1986, I received the Mayor's Liberty Medal from Mayor Ed Koch of New York, which was awarded to foreigners who had made major contributions to the city and the country. Dancer and choreographer Mikhail Baryshnikov was among the awardees, as were the Russian poet Joseph Brodsky, the Canadian businessman and publisher Mort Zuckerman, and the Israeli author and sex psychologist Dr. Ruth Westheimer. The award was a big deal, but I knew Alain wouldn't want me to go to the ceremony in New York, so I didn't. When I got the telegram from Mayor Koch, rather than being able to enjoy it and show it off and go to America to collect the award, I played it down and asked my mother to go and collect it for me.

My relationship with Sears suffered irreparable damage. It was clear that Alain did not want me to go to Chicago to meet with Sears when I was supposed to. I canceled a lot of appointments and some appearances and became so unreliable that Sears did not renew our contract.

My couture collection also foundered because I wasn't paying the attention to it I should have. My concept of expensive designer clothes and an elegant designer bou-

tique had been right and would be a forerunner of the many others that would appear in the 1980s. It was just the timing in my personal life that was difficult. I eventually sold the lease on the boutique in New York to Geoffrey Beene. My couture line vanished because it was sold only there.

In retrospect, these mistakes in professional judgment were probably inevitable. I had turned a page when I moved to Paris and was neglecting all things in America. I was very high on Europe at the time, and by choice my priority was my personal life. No one was forcing me to stay in Paris, after all. It was my choice.

Alain and I spent a good deal of time in Capri, where we rented a small apartment in the old part of town. I've always liked Italian villages and was very happy there going for fresh bread and the newspaper in the morning while Alain was writing. Moravia was often with us in Capri, and while they were working on the biography, I followed Italian politics and culture.

At a gala dinner organized by the fashion house Fendi we went to in Rome at the Palazzo Venezia in 1985, we sipped champagne on the balcony from which Mussolini had declared war and had dinner in the room that had been his office. Among the guests in the Renaissance palazzo were American and European journalists who were smiling behind the signature fans designed by Karl Lagerfeld.

The fashion world of the 1980s was booming, fueled by the increasing importance of brand names. The Fendi sisters had enlarged the family business from designing beautiful furs to making everything from luggage to swimwear, and the House of Chanel was being revitalized by Lagerfeld as well.

New designers were making their mark. Gianni Versace was rising quickly, as was Giorgio Armani, who had gone from being a window dresser to reinventing Italian fashion. In the United States Donna Karan was on the rise, taking over where I had left off.

It was very interesting being in Rome with Alain and all of a sudden being back in the fashion world for a night. I knew all the fashion journalists there. Two of my lives were intersecting, and I felt a little pang. It was so easy for me to talk to my journalist friends, and I could see that fashion was taking a big leap ahead in the same period that I was not being active in it. It was a weird feeling. I felt both superior and inferior, attached and detached. On the one hand, I felt quite smug that I'd been there, done that, and moved on. On the other hand, other designers were doing fashion and I wasn't.

But fashion was not in my cards then. I had made a brief attempt to design clothes in Paris. I asked the now-famous designer Hervé Léger to help me, and we did a small, elegant fashion show in my apartment. The clothes were jersey dresses, somewhat like the original jersey dress but with a more French look and all in solid colors. I sold the clothes at a boutique called Victoire and at Au Printemps, a department store in Paris, and the line did well. But I did it for only one season. I quickly lost interest because I didn't want to get back into a real business.

I was on the periphery of the fashion world, a designer with a successful track record who was not currently designing anything of her own. Though I remained on *Savvy* magazine's survey list of the top ten United States businesses run by women for the entire five years I was in Paris (1984 to

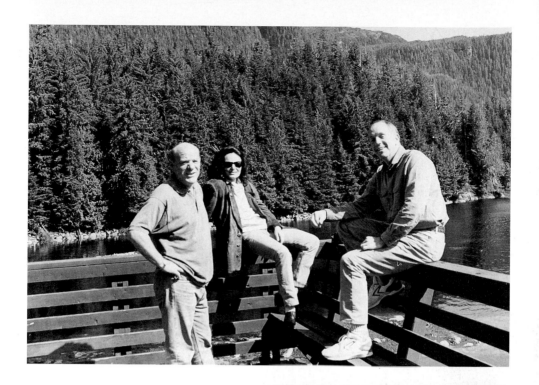

Herb Allen, the famous investment
banker and a true American
gentleman, invited Barry and me to
join him fishing for salmon in
Alaska. Here we are on the terrace
at the lodge.

One of my favorite photos of
Barry, just as I see him . . . warm
and loving.

Barry and I photographed by Annie Leibovitz in his New York apartment for *Vanity Fair*'s 1993 Hall of Fame. (*Annie Leibovitz,* Vanity Fair)

My daughter, Tatiana, photographed by Richard Avedon at the Volpi Ball in Venice in 1991. *(Richard Avedon, Egoïste)*

My son Alexandre. *(David Mickelek)*

With my nieces, Kelly and Sarah, my brother Philippe's daughters, in my office on their first trip to New York. I take pride in being "the aunt from America."

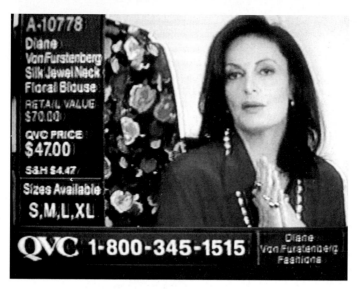

On the air for the 1992 launch of *Silk Assets* on QVC.
(Jacques M. Chenet/Gamma Liaison)

Karl Lagerfeld was very intrigued by the concept of electronic retailing. He made this drawing of me "seeing into the future" of TV shopping.

Moguls at rest. Barry, Calvin, David Geffen, and Sandy Gallin on a cruise in the Bahamas. A favorite picture from one of the many cruises we all took together. *(Kelly Klein)*

My series of books on the home: *Beds*; *The Bath*; and *The Table*.
(Stewart O'Shields)

My first day of radiation treatment in May 1994. I dressed in bright
colors because I didn't want to look sad. I was actually very afraid and I
wondered if I would look the same after treatment.

Meeting Fidel Castro in
Havana, Cuba, on a trip with
Mort Zuckerman in 1993. I
was quite impressed by him.

Attending President Clinton's
first state dinner at the White
House (for the Emperor and
Empress of Japan), wearing
John Galliano. (*Official White
House photo*)

Reading time. Sailing with Barry in St. Lucia.

Isabel Liscano, my friend from school in Switzerland.

A reunion with my first boss, photo agent Albert Koski.

Marisa Berenson, my friend and companion of many years.

With Nona Gordon Summers on her
birthday.

Bianca Kermonvant, my friend and
"healer," with her son, Julien.

With Christian Louboutin, a very
talented French shoe designer. I met him
only recently, but he has become one of
my best friends. Here we are in his shop
in Paris.

Friends Jane Wenner and Hugo
Jereissati.

My friend Marina Schiano took this photo of Alex and Alex on their wedding day, October 28, 1995. It is one of my favorite photographs of the two of them; they look so happy. Alexandra looked beautiful in her gown designed by Karl Lagerfeld. *(Marina Schiano)*

At the wedding reception with Egon, sharing feelings of disbelief that our son is actually getting married. *(Marina Schiano)*

My brother and my mother arriving at the wedding reception. *(Marina Schiano)*

The new extended family. *(Eric Boman)*

My mother with Mireille von Hannover, my first childhood friend.

Friends Dolly Parton and Fran Lebowitz at the reception. *(Marina Schiano)*

Tatiana, Alex, and I at the 1997 VH1
Fashion Awards. (W)

Models, including me, wearing my dresses
in every window of my new headquarters
in Greenwich Village! Ever since I bought
this building, I have dreamed of this
shot . . . and here it is. Todd Eberle
photographed this for *Vanity Fair*, but
this snapshot was taken by one of my
associates as we were setting up.

Alexandra and I at work. *(Philip Greenberg, The New York Times)*

1989), every time I went to New York, I got more and more depressed.

The licensees did not want even to listen to my ideas or see my designs. As a result, many of the salesmen didn't understand the philosophy behind the products I had designed and often didn't know how to sell them. Instead, they had resorted more and more to copying what somebody else was selling in order to boost sales. In the process, many of our original product designs had changed so much that they bore no relationship to what had forged the basis for the license in the first place. My name was on the products, but the products had little or nothing to do with me. In the mid- and late eighties. I was less a fashion contender than a cash cow for others.

The bonus of not having to work so hard was the time I had to travel. During one school vacation, I took the children to Russia, where they traded music tapes for army belts with Russian teenagers at the Pushkin Fine Arts Museum in Moscow. On other vacations, Alain and I took his children and mine to ski in the Swiss Alps and to tour Egypt. We were a family, and my relationship with Alain was like a marriage. I loved his children, and they became close to mine. To this day, I talk to them and see them as often as possible.

For the Christmas holidays of 1986, I rented a chalet for all of us in Gstaad, where I spent a memorable birthday, my thirty-ninth. We all went to a New Year's Eve party Valentino was giving in his chalet, and my dinner partner turned out to be Frank Sinatra. When the inevitable birthday cake was presented to me, Frank Sinatra raised his glass and sang "Happy Birthday." My fortieth birthday the next year was no less memorable. We went to Israel, where I had my

birthday lunch at the president's residence with Chaim Herzog and his wife, Aura, whom I had met when they had been posted at the United Nations in New York.

We spent some of the children's vacations in America. One summer we rented a house in Amagansett, a village in the Hamptons on Long Island. My children were at their teenage worst and very annoying, which may contribute to my somewhat negative attitude toward the Hamptons. The summer scene was very social, and there were too many people playing country. I far preferred Connecticut, where the village near Cloudwalk was simpler and more honest.

The fast-track life in the Hamptons was symptomatic of a larger shift that began occurring in the 1980s. During my monthly visits to New York, I watched the social ethos change. Andy Warhol died in 1987, and the flamboyant, artistic spirits at his funeral at St. Patrick's Cathedral, such as Viva, Ultra Violet, and Pat Ast, seemed like ghosts from another era. When we gathered afterward at the old ballroom that had once been Billy Rose's Diamond Horseshoe, the darkness of the room made me think of Studio 54, which had also closed.

CHRISTIAN LACROIX was the new fashion craze. Financed by Bernard Arnault, who now owns Dior and is the leading fashion mogul of the world, Lacroix's arrival in New York created a stir. His lavish clothes were the epitome of the eighties; they screamed money. Ivana and Donald Trump were in the first row of the fashion show Christian put on in 1987 at the newly built World Financial Center in Battery Park City. Sitting there, I remembered the last time I had

been in nearby Battery Park, it had been an open field and Jane Fonda had been demonstrating for peace while the crowd smoked pot.

For the first time I was very much aware of the passage of time. To have been successful at such a young age had always been central to my identity and had given me a sense of arrogance. I had been so focused when I turned thirty, at forty I wasn't sure where I stood as a woman or as a professional anymore. When I had met Alain, I had been convinced that I no longer wanted to be a businesswoman. I wanted to write and I did make a few attempts, but I felt inadequate to write a book. I spent a good deal of time in Paris writing in my diaries. I began to feel insecure.

Creating a literary salon was amusing. The translations I did for Salvy were stimulating. But I am not a writer. I was helping other people do what they do best, while I was surely not doing what I do best. I had given up my business for a new life with Alain, but now I wasn't sure.

ALAIN EMBARKED upon an affair with a friend of mine, and I found myself in a situation I had not experienced before. I was shaken and very hurt. Who was I? I had turned my back on the strong identity I had forged in America, where I had a life and career of my own. And here I was in Paris, devoting my life to a man who had betrayed me. For weeks I walked the streets of Paris like a lost soul, not knowing what to do. It was very painful.

Should a woman ever give up her life for a man? I kept asking myself. Egon had once asked me to do that. At some point he had said, "Either you give me your business, or

we separate." And I had replied, "Okay, we'll separate." But we had been very young then, still children really. But now I was a forty-year-old woman, and the question wouldn't go away unanswered.

Alain had said he hated my leopard carpets and the violent colors I wore when he met me. But I realized that in the end, that was what he had liked in me. I began to understand the universal truth—rather late—that when a woman loses the power of her own personality, she loses what attracted the man to her in the first place. She becomes the docile, passive person she thinks he wants, and then he is attracted by another shiny person. That's exactly what had happened to me.

For the first time, I found myself in competition with a woman I knew well. I was angry with her and with Alain, but I decided not to leave him. The affair stopped but there were others. And then I moved on.

After four and a half years in Paris, I was being called back by America. My children were calling me back. Cloudwalk was calling me back. So was my work. For all the good times I had had in Paris, there was an emptiness to my life. And my love for Alain had stopped growing.

I realize now that all the men I've loved have fit into something I needed at the time. Beyond being in love with the person, I was also in love with a lifestyle, a situation, and the person was a major part of that situation. At the moment Alain had appeared in my life, he had represented the change I craved most, just as Paulo, who returned to Bali after we broke up, had five years before. Barry, too, had been a symbol of my early tycoon years, but in that case our relationship changed and continued to grow. The men I've loved—and

the situations—could not have been more different, but they were all part of my personality. With my obsession for turning negatives into positives and having little memory for pain, I arrange and rearrange my life not always knowing if it is by design or by adapting to the situation.

The end with Alain came abruptly. I was in New York in 1989 when I had a problem with a tooth and the dentist said he would have to pull it. So, I thought, with the tooth goes my life in Paris. I came back to America. I had no idea how difficult the reentry would be.

THE HARD ROAD
HOME

CONFRONTING the degraded status of the brand was very hard. The fashion license had been sold from one company to another and the distribution broadened so much that my name had sunk to the bottom of the retail pool and the clothes had absolutely nothing to do with me. The licensed line of children's clothes, for example, had descended into tacky, overdone dresses with too many bows. The label had lost its coherence.

The disintegration of the cosmetics company was even more painful. When I had sold the beauty and fragrance division to Beecham in 1983, the company had had excellent distribution with great location in the department stores. Then Beecham, originally a pharmaceuticals company, had decided it shouldn't be in cosmetics after all and had sold off the companies it had acquired.

The *Color Authority* cosmetics line vanished during the mergers and acquisitions that followed. *Tatiana* fragrance, the sole survivor, was bought by Revlon in 1988, but was soon unrecognizable. One of Revlon's marketing people decided to turn the juice purple to launch the scent in Europe. When I went to the launches in London and Paris in 1989, the new *Tatiana* looked more like nail polish remover than the light, sexy scent it had once been.

The purpling of *Tatiana* is what happens when some marketing person who does not understand the philosophy behind a product decides that he or she knows how to sell the product better than the person who created it. Revlon was also interested in volume, so it distributed *Tatiana* to mass merchants and drugstores but failed to support it with advertising. Within a few years, my name had become a "brand at risk."

I was depressed. Some days I would go to my office, stare out the window, and wonder what I was doing there. I still had a few licenses—the awful children's line as well as stationery, a fashion line in Mexico, nurses' uniforms, luggage, and eyewear—and I tried to breathe life back into them. I made a personal appearance at a convention in Las Vegas for the eyewear license and suggested a leopard and tiger print for the stationery. I also designed some successful tapestry patterns for the luggage. But the overall picture was bleak.

When I moved to Paris, I had been making more than $4 million a year from royalties. By the time I returned five years later, that income had dropped by around 75 percent. The quality and the distribution of the licensed products, which had generated well over $1 billion in retail sales in the prior decade, had deteriorated. There were useless, frustrating meetings at my office with the licensees, but they weren't paying much attention to anything I said.

I still had my beautiful office on Fifth Avenue, although the overall space was down to a third of its original size. The rent had become exorbitant, the building had changed management, and Jann Wenner and *Rolling Stone* had long since moved out. I clung to my reduced office space like

the branch of a tree I'd once had. The atmosphere of the building, and of the city itself, had changed.

I had been out of touch with the rhythms of New York life for almost ten years, and for the first few months after my return, I wasn't sure where or if I fit in. The whole world seemed unfamiliar. I followed the Gulf War on television with my Italian friend Roffredo, and could not believe the sight of Isaac Stern playing violin at a concert in Jerusalem while wearing a gas mask.

I tried to reconnect with my old life. I had lots of lunches in the Grill Room at the Four Seasons, where the major players in New York congregate. I renewed my friendship with Mort Zuckerman, a real estate developer and editor in chief of *U.S. News & World Report* and *The Atlantic*, who would soon acquire the New York *Daily News*. I saw a lot of Calvin and Kelly Klein, Fran Lebowitz, and David Geffen, my old friend who by now had become a major entertainment industry powerhouse. I saw a lot of Jann and Jane Wenner; *Rolling Stone* had also grown into a large media conglomerate. I made new friends too. *Spy* magazine was a pertinent voice that was making good fun of the garish new affluence in New York and I became good friends with its editor, Graydon Carter, and his family.

Once again, the only place I felt truly comfortable was at home at Cloudwalk, and I returned there with relief. The children were both at Brown University and in very good hands. Vartan Gregorian, one of the people I most admire in New York, had left the stewardship of the New York Public Library to become president of Brown. His liberal, open-minded generosity and his appetite for knowledge had always impressed me. Tatiana and Alexandre would

bring their friends home on weekends. Now it was I who drew strength from the children, of whom I was very proud. Being back in America also put me closer to Barry, who as always was strong, loyal, and reassuring. So, slowly, I began to readjust.

For the first time in close to ten years I wasn't living with a man, and I found I enjoyed it. Though I was struggling to reclaim my professional identity as a person, as a woman, I was free. And I took advantage of it. I traveled.

In the summer of 1989, I went to Malcolm Forbes's seventieth birthday extravaganza in Morocco, which was as much a celebration of the decade's glorification of capitalism as it was of him. I sat on the railing of *Midnight Saga*, the huge yacht rented for the occasion by Australian media tycoon Rupert Murdoch, and watched the intermingling of the new society: Robert Maxwell, the British media baron and union buster; Jimmy Goldschmidt, the British corporate raider; and Henry Kravis, the czar of leveraged corporate takeovers in New York, sipping champagne with Elizabeth Taylor and Forbes. I would have preferred to visit author Paul Bowles, who lived in Tangier, but I was with a very different group of people and had a perfectly nice time.

In the fall of 1989, I went to Germany, where I witnessed the fall of the Berlin Wall. The sound of hundreds of hammers chipping away at the Wall was like the victory peal of a hundred church bells. As almost everybody else who was there, I brought home pieces of the colorful, graffiti-covered Wall in my pockets.

I attended another celebration of freedom, this one for Václav Havel, the new president of democratic Czecho-slovakia. Havel's friend and mine, Milos Forman, orches-

trated an event at the Cathedral of St. John the Divine in New York. With two thousand others who packed the huge space, we lit candles and were given little bells to symbolize freedom. My little bell is still attached to one of my traveling bags.

Inspired by Havel, who said at dinner at the Vivian Beaumont Theater at Lincoln Center later that night, "The first lie spoken in the name of truth is the beginning of the end," I decided to go to Czechoslovakia. Alain, who had remained my close friend, came with me on that trip, and we spent a week visiting Kafka's tomb and walking through the Jewish cemetery in Prague.

I went to China, Japan, Sri Lanka, and Turkey, and drove around Spain. It was with great delight that I accepted an invitation from Mort to accompany him to Cuba, where we spent two days with Fidel Castro. He was tall and handsome, with piercing eyes. He was charming and spoke at length, asking us many questions about America. A lawyer by training, he is very intelligent and I found him extremely informed, but somehow he was not quite as macho as I had expected. At the end of our visit, I wasn't sure if I liked him or not. I did, however, continue to admire him for his loyalty to his cause. "Your mother really picked the right name for you," I told him on our last evening, *fidel* meaning "faithful" in Spanish. He was amused by my comment but confessed that his mother had named him Fidel because she was hoping that a very rich landowner they knew named Fidel would be his godfather. It hadn't happened, but he had kept the name and its meaning.

□

THERE WAS a new excitement everywhere in 1992. Graydon Carter became editor of *Vanity Fair* when Tina Brown moved to *The New Yorker,* and the first thing he did was to put me on the masthead as a contributing editor. One of my first assignments was to cover the couture collections in Paris. I had done it once before, in the summer of 1989 on assignment for Shelley Wanger, the editor of *Interview* magazine. It had been interesting being on the other side of the desk and working with Greek artist Konstantin Kakanias, who illustrated the article I wrote. As a designer, I was reassured to find that the clothes were extravagant, expensive, and in the indulgent mode I had forecast in my own collection five years before. But while it was comforting to know that my instincts had been right, it was disturbing to realize how removed I had become from the fashion world while I had been living in Paris; while I had let my made-to-order line fade away, I hadn't even bothered keeping up with the other couture collections. Sometimes I can't believe the odd way I run my life.

A few of us from the magazine went to Washington for Bill Clinton's inauguration in January 1993. I had first met Clinton with Barry at the Democratic National Convention. I immediately liked him. I liked the fact that he had been a Rhodes scholar, that Gabriel García Márquez is his favorite novelist, that he always appears on the good side of things, and that we are the same age. Besides, as we all know now, he is totally charming and he has a way of talking to you that makes you feel you are the only person he wants to see.

For the first time I was inspired to become an American citizen. I got all the papers and forms but was so overwhelmed when I came to the section that asked me to list

each trip I had taken out of the United States in the last twenty years that I gave up. Reconstructing the hundreds of trips I had taken was just too much.

I felt great at the big inaugural bash we went to for Clinton at the Capitol Center. Former president Jimmy Carter was there, as were Washington insiders such as Vernon Jordan, presidential children such as John F. Kennedy Jr. eating a hot dog with Daryl Hannah, entertainers such as Michael Jackson and Aretha Franklin, who was hardly politically correct in her huge mink stole but who sang divinely, and many, many Hollywood stars: Warren Beatty and Annette Bening, Hollywood's royal couple; Her Highness Barbra Streisand, who sang and preached; Goldie Hawn, Sally Field, and Macaulay Culkin, all wearing little red ribbons for AIDS awareness, the first time I saw so many of them at a public event.

IN NEW YORK, I had time now to get involved in causes I cared about. I helped raise money for the National Holocaust Museum, which was being built in Washington, D.C. I went with my mother to a fund-raiser at the French Embassy in Washington, and I gave a small fund-raising dinner myself in New York. I invited the Wenners, Calvin Klein, Alberto Vitale (the chairman of Random House), and a few other prominent Jews. But I hate asking anyone for money, and I become incredibly emotional when talking about the Holocaust. I was so distressed that evening that I can't remember much about it, certainly not how much money was raised. But I forced myself to seek support for the museum because I thought it was important.

It would be quite a revenge for my mother and me to attend its inauguration in Washington in April 1993, accompanied by my children, Alexandre and Tatiana. I held her small hand tightly as we walked quickly through the original gate of Auschwitz with its sign ARBEIT MACHT FREI. I did not want her to break down. The four of us were silent as we walked through the museum, keeping our feelings under control. My mother's example had taught us not to give in to sorrow but always to try to celebrate life instead. We went off to an Italian restaurant, happy to be together, turning the day from darkness to light. However, it took all of us several days to recover from this experience.

I STARTED SLOWLY to reconnect to the world of design by finishing a book I'd started in Paris entitled *Beds.* The inspirational decorating book, with beautiful color photographs of some 170 beds in villas, apartments, and lofts all over the world, was a joint venture with my friend Olivier, who designed it. I felt somewhat responsible for him because he had managed the now-defunct boutique at the Sherry Netherland. We would do two other books—*The Bath* in 1994 and *The Table* in 1996.

"We all do the same things; what makes us different is how we do it" had been one of my mother's dicta. We all sleep, bathe, and eat. With these books, I tried to pay attention to daily rituals and celebrate them aesthetically by photographing the most beautiful decors I could find. It was a satisfying project, but I was still going through a very difficult time.

I spent countless hours with Revlon, which owned

what was left of my name in beauty and fragrance, trying to create a product line that did not compete with something they already had so I would become important to them. But trying to establish myself within this huge company proved to be futile. I went from one marketing director to another, trying to spark a fire, but couldn't.

I didn't realize how depressed I was until a weekend I spent in the summer of 1990 with Kelly and Calvin Klein. Calvin was recovering from a terrible horseback-riding accident he had had in the Hamptons. I had been in the Hamptons visiting Jane and Jann Wenner when I had heard about Calvin's accident, and I had immediately driven to meet his wife. I flew with her in a helicopter to New York, where he had been taken to a hospital, and we've been much closer friends since.

Later that summer, Barry and I were together with Calvin and David Geffen when the conversation turned to work and suddenly I started to cry. They were all talking about what they were doing, and I realized I had no business at all. Calvin, who was having difficulties with his own business at the time, was especially sympathetic. I drew great inspiration from him, watching him rebuild his health while rebuilding his business.

My accountant was somber. The world had changed, he kept telling me; the way to go was toward the mass market and license my name to, say, a chain like Wal-Mart. He cared most about the income; I cared most about the product.

In spite of my misgivings, I explored the possibilities, which only depressed me more. Like my accountant, the manufacturers I talked to encouraged me to sign licensing agreements with them and to go mass market. Financially

that made sense, of course. I went to visit some Wal-Mart stores, but as much as I appreciated the strength and the power of the huge megastores, I found it difficult to imagine how I could fit in at that level of the market. Besides, I knew that if I were to go that way, I would never be able to get back into the better stores. Everyone was polite, but it was quite clear from their looks and the way they talked to me that they considered me something of a has-been.

I ended up signing a licensing deal with a public company called Russ Togs in 1990 to establish a separate DVF division. It was my first attempt to get back into fashion, but I did it with very little conviction. The parent company was not doing well, and its lack of direction combined with my lack of enthusiasm was not exactly a winning proposition. Though I knew the company was banking on my name to solve some of its own problems, I went ahead anyway because it would get me back into retail stores.

I was uncomfortable, however, with the quality of the moderate sportswear line I helped Russ Togs design. We had to settle for lower quality in their price range, and I was unhappy about it. I was marginally happier with the dresses I went on to design in 1991, clever woven wrap tops and stretch woven skirts that looked like separates. The fabric wasn't what I wished it could be, but finally there was a product that I could somewhat identify with. The day the DVF division was to launch the line, Russ Togs declared bankruptcy.

I had worked hard on the new dresses, which were interesting and nice, and for the first time in almost two years, I had an entree back into the stores. Without thinking for one second, I told the people I'd been working with at Russ Togs to move the dresses to my office and come work

directly for me. "We'll do this ourselves," I told them. One of them, supersmart Kathy Landau, became a key player in my comeback later.

So I was back in the dress business with an inherited staff and an inherited dress line that I was neither sure how to operate nor really wanted to operate. We showed the dresses in the fall of 1991 and got a few orders from department stores, but my heart wasn't in it. The fabric wasn't good enough, and the dresses weren't well made. Although they would debut quite successfully at Macy's in the spring of 1992 and we would have all the windows on Herald Square for the launch, I pulled the plug. I didn't want to get myself back into manufacturing. And I was on the verge of an unexpected breakthrough.

I HAD BEEN on my way to Paris in the summer of 1991 when I ran into Joe Spellman, the marketing genius for Elizabeth Arden and Unilever, in the Concorde lounge at JFK. I was on my way to Venice for the debutante ball of Elizabeth de Balkany, the granddaughter of the former king of Italy, that count Giovanni Volpi was giving for her in his palace. I was very much looking forward to it, mostly because my twenty-year-old daughter was going to be there. I had been only slightly older than Tatiana when Egon and I had gone to another Volpi ball two decades earlier.

I still carried the memories of the gondolas dropping off the debutantes and titled young men at the torchlit palace on the Grand Canal. The women all looked beautiful, helped by the makeup artists and hairdressers who had been flown in from Paris, including Alexandre de Paris, who took three

suites at the Bauer Grünwald hotel. Now it would be my daughter's turn to experience her first Venetian ball and be a young beauty herself in a gray lace dress made by her father, who had become a couture designer in Rome. For me, however, the encounter with Joe Spellman at the airport had a special beauty of its own.

"Diane, if you wanted, you could have the biggest name in the new millennium," he told me as we waited for the plane. I was flattered, and since I respected his marketing intuition, I was intrigued. Gradually an interesting idea for a new partnership began to take shape.

Joe got in touch with Lester Gribbetz, a wizard in home furnishings and the former cochairman of Bloomingdale's, who got in touch with Marvin Traub, a wizard in fashion and the flamboyant former chairman of Bloomingdale's. I would meet to explore rebuilding my brand as partners with these three wizards. They agreed that I had had an important name in fashion and offered to create a new venture that would build it into a new brand. My potential partners were experts in the three fields in which I had once excelled: fashion, beauty, and home. I was really excited at the prospect.

But there was a little part of me that kept asking: This is all well and good, but is the partnership right for me? The three men were all consultants, very involved with other businesses. We were talking about creating the new company as equal partners, which meant the profits would be split four ways while I would end up doing most of the work.

I went along with the discussions, however, because I felt it was the best option I had at the time and might lead somewhere. And it did. It was Joe Spellman who brought up

the idea at one of our meetings in the winter of 1992. "How about selling on television?" he asked.

I KNEW THE MOMENT that I walked into the QVC studio in West Chester, Pennsylvania, that I had found an answer. It was February 29, leap year, and the four of us had taken the Metroliner down from New York to see the operation. QVC was popularly dismissed as tacky by the retail establishment in New York for selling "collectibles" such as faux vintage dolls and model cars, but my friend Kenny Lane and TV-star-turned-jewelry-designer Joan Rivers were supposedly reaping windfalls on television. True to form, Marvin joked as we toured the studio, but I saw a golden opportunity. As I followed the three men down the corridor, I found myself thinking aloud, "I want to own this place."

Susan Lucci, the soap opera actress, happened to be on the air selling hair products when we arrived. To our amazement, we watched the sales mount on the computer to $600,000.

Susan was doing what I had been doing for years. Talking directly to women through a television camera was like making a personal appearance on a national level. The setting was more removed, but the format would allow me to reopen a dialogue with women. And the market was already in place.

With malls taking over America, home shopping essentially brought a television mall into everybody's home, store by store. And the audience seemed to take to it. In only five years of operation, this home shopping channel had amassed forty-two million viewers, three million of whom

were regular shoppers. Teleshopping was a new and interesting way of selling, and I wanted to try it.

Unlike the discouraging manufacturers and retailers I'd talked to, Darlene Daggett, the force behind QVC's fashion merchandising department, was eager to talk to me. She wanted personal appearances by well-known fashion designers like me to attract a more sophisticated audience. I, in turn, needed an audience. All that remained was coming up with the concept and working out a contract.

Developing a line of clothes to sell on television was daunting at first. I had never designed clothes that women couldn't first try on. I decided to return to an idea that I had had before but never developed: a line of silk pieces called *Silk Assets*—dresses, pants, skirts, blazers, and tops—that were tied together by prints and coordinating colors. The tops would be big shirts, tank tops, and tunics, cut generously enough to be worn in different ways; the pants and skirts would have somewhat elasticized waists. But who would make them?

My partners, it was turning out, did not want to commit to buying inventory. The partnership, in fact, was beginning to come apart. Barry was acting as my business adviser, and at a meeting at his office at Fox in New York, my would-be partners announced they would not be involved in the apparel line at all. "That's okay," I said. "I'll do it myself."

I was relieved. I remember dancing out on the street after the meeting and feeling free. I already had an idea as to how I could have the clothes manufactured and not have any inventory responsibilities.

"This is what we could do," I told Darlene Daggett. "I will design the clothes. I will source them by finding and

supervising the right manufacturer, make sure that you get the shipment on time and that the quality is right. But when the time comes to open the letter of credit to buy the merchandise from the factory and bring it in, you will do it. The factory in Hong Kong will ship directly to you, and you will own the inventory. That way, by going direct, you will be able to take a generous markup for yourselves and give the customer fantastic quality and a fabulous price." My compensation, I told her, would be 25 percent on top of cost. By Monday morning, we had a deal. And I went off to the Orient to have the clothes made.

Once again I was stepping off into the unknown, but, to my amazement, so was Barry. We were on our way to Cloudwalk from the airport after one of my first trips to the Far East to find a factory when he announced abruptly that he was thinking of leaving Fox. I was absolutely astounded. He had such an incredible success in his seven years at Fox since leaving Paramount. Though everyone had said it was impossible to create a fourth network, he had. But Barry, who was turning fifty and reevaluating his own life and career, had finally realized that Fox wasn't his and never would be. Fox was owned by Rupert Murdoch, who had his own dynastic family—and the company was theirs.

"What are you going to do?" I asked him. "I don't know," he said. He had just gotten a laptop computer, and he used it for the first time to draft the announcement of his resignation from Fox. The announcement would go through countless editing with my insistence that he keep it short and unsentimental. Then he took his laptop and set off to drive around America, where he started thinking about new ways to use digital communication. So Barry, too, was looking for

a new opportunity at the same time I was about to realize one of my own.

I SOLD OUT the entire collection of *Silk Assets* in my debut on QVC in November 1992—$1.3 million dollars in just two hours. There was enormous excitement on the set. Along with the cheering people there from my office was Kate Betts, a new, young, clever editor at *Vogue* who had come to observe the debut. Her article, "Show and Sell," would begin, "*Vogue* witnesses a fashion phenomenon in the making."

There was just as much excitement backstage in the greenroom, where Barry and all the top management of QVC had watched the galloping volume of sales on a computer and cheered as if they were at the races. What they didn't know was that while *Silk Assets* was being manufactured during the summer of 1992, Barry had begun negotiations with QVC's major stockholders—Comcast and Brian and Ralph Roberts. It would soon be announced that he had taken control of the home shopping network. I would be part of the business. Because I had introduced Barry to QVC, I got 10 percent of his share. Besides all the other things we were to each other, we were now business partners as well.

Together we launched the entire teleshopping indus-try into orbit. Between Barry's involvement and my success, the shopping network was all over the front pages. Suddenly I went from has-been to pioneer again.

For Barry, however, the transition from being the head of Fox to QVC was odd and somewhat unpredictable. I felt terribly guilty although amused on the first day he was in his new office at this new company that was selling fake

diamond rings when he called me and asked, "Could you please tell me what I am doing here?" But there was a lot of excitement. Everyone who was anyone was coming to visit the operation in Pennsylvania and talking about electronic retailing.

They couldn't stock enough of my silk separates. On one show in 1993, I would sell 2,200 pairs of silk trousers in less than two minutes. On another night, at midnight, I sold $750,000 worth of merchandise in just fifteen minutes. In the four good years I would spend on that home shopping channel, Silk Assets would generate more than $40 million in sales.

As the apparel line did well on television, there were finally stirrings of interest at Revlon about an idea I'd come up with for a new environmental fragrance line. The basic concept of the line, which we would call *Surroundings*, was to bring the beauty of the garden indoors in the form of a candle, an air spray, a soap, body lotion, and a hair and body shampoo.

Just as *Surroundings* was about to be launched, however, Revlon decided to unload everything that was not under the Revlon brand. *Surroundings* was doomed, but Revlon's decision to consolidate was an opportunity for me. Having sold the trademark for my fragrance and beauty business to Beecham in 1983 for $22 million, I would buy it back from Revlon a decade later for $250,000.

IN 1994, BARRY AND I decided to create a second, more upscale home shopping channel, Q2, based in New York. A lot of high-end designers were interested. Karl Lagerfeld was

intrigued by the idea of Q2, and I spent a lot of time with him in Paris discussing it. He made me a little drawing of my face looking into a crystal ball that says "TV for 1994." Gianni Versace called me after hearing about teleshopping from John Fairchild at *Women's Wear Daily*, and I went to see Gianni at the St. Regis. The lunch date I made with Ralph Lauren in 1994 to explore his selling on television, however, would end up in a very different exploration.

I didn't know Ralph that well, and it was only through professional courtesy, I'm sure, that he agreed to have lunch with me. But our conversation grew intimate after I finished my appeal about Q2. He started to tell me about his life, and in the process, probably saved mine.

THE YEAR BEFORE, Ralph had been diagnosed with a brain tumor that had turned out to be benign. I asked him over lunch what his symptoms had been. He told me he had heard this little noise in his ear that wouldn't go away, so he had gone to an ear doctor. The doctor had found nothing wrong but had ordered an MRI and discovered the tumor.

As I listened to Ralph, I realized that I, too, had a noise in my ear. I had paid no attention to it, but when the next day I heard the noise again, I asked my friend, Dr. Isador Rosenfeld, to refer me to an ear doctor. The ear specialist, like Ralph's, found nothing the matter with my ear, but he did notice a swollen gland in my neck. Had I had a cold, he asked? I had not. It's probably nothing, he said and put me on antibiotics for a week. But the swollen gland didn't go away.

Dr. Rosenfeld was anxious that the gland was still

swollen and ordered further tests. The ear doctor I'd seen first was on vacation, so he sent me to a head and neck doctor at Memorial Sloan Kettering Cancer Center, one of the world's leading cancer hospitals. That doctor suggested that we give the antibiotics another week to work, and if the gland was still swollen, he would do a biopsy. I wanted to know the outcome right away, however, so I could begin to deal with it. "Where do you do the biopsy?" I asked him. "Right here in the office," he said. "So why not do the biopsy now?" I asked him. He did, and again, the signs were optimistic. He drew fluid from the gland, which signaled that the swelling came from a cyst. "That probably means that it's nothing, but we'll send the fluid to be tested," he said.

The tests came back normal. But the gland, which had gone down, swelled again. The doctor kept assuring me that the tests were normal, it was just a cyst. There was no hurry in removing it. I could do it in six months, a year. But I was getting annoyed. "I want to do it right away," I said. They operated on Friday, May 13. The cyst they removed looked normal. It was not until they cut into it that they discovered tiny, tiny bad cells that had already metastasized. Tatiana, my mother, and Barry were with me at the hospital. Everyone was in shock and silent. Alexandre, who was working in Hong Kong at the time, punched a wall when he heard the news. He got sixteen stitches on his hand and jumped onto the first plane for New York. Dr. Rosenfeld took charge. Where was the source of the cancer?

Again they operated and, after scraping my throat, found the answer: tiny cancerous cells at the base of my tongue and in my soft palate. I would have to undergo eight weeks of radiation treatment.

I was afraid of radiation. There was enough risk in having an X ray, and subjecting my body to radiation was more dangerous by far. I considered alternatives, and after my friend Sandy Gallin told me that Deepak Chopra was lecturing in Connecticut, I invited him to Cloudwalk. Chopra, an endocrinologist and influential New Age healer who stresses the power of love and energy (he has sold more than ten million books in thirty languages), came to Cloudwalk on a Friday night and taught me how to meditate. He also invited me out to the Chopra Center for Well Being in La Jolla, California, an invitation I accepted. Tatiana was with me the first two days. Her presence was warm and reassuring but I was also eager to be alone. I took long walks on the beach, looking at the horizon, questioning the future, meditating, praying, and finding strength in myself. By the time I had gone to California however, I had already decided I was going to do the radiation. The only question was how best to deal with it.

Rather than surrender to the disease or put myself too much into the hands of others, I decided to take the treatment into my own hands and develop my own regimen to confront it. My recipe was to focus on what was wrong, to look for whatever help I felt was right, and somehow to put it all together into a single cocktail, my own. In the process, I drew on healing techniques I learned from Chopra and other healers, from homeopathic medicine, from rituals I invented, and from my own powers of concentration. The critical ingredient for me was to believe in that regimen and go for it. And so I found my way through the treatment.

I designed a strict routine during the eight weeks of radiation. I went to Sloan Kettering every day at 1 P.M. but

often had to wait a long time in the waiting room for the radiation. I chose a very thick book, *Wild Swans* by Jung Chang, to read only during the waiting period at the hospital. I drew great strength from the story of this Chinese mother, daughter, and granddaughter, each of whom surmounted the horrors of her generation and fought for freedom on her own terms. The book seemed not only the right content but also the right length. I figured that by the time I finished it, the treatment would be over, and it was.

I made a great effort to look well when I went to the hospital. I did my hair and my makeup more carefully than I usually do and dressed in bright, positive colors. On the first day I was scheduled for radiation, I took a photograph of myself in the mirror in my bathroom, wondering what I would look like at the end of the treatment.

I usually had a driver in New York, but I decided that I would walk the eighteen blocks between my office and Sloan Kettering every day. I never allowed anyone to come with me or be there with me. It was something I wanted to deal with by myself. My son came for the first visit with the radiologist to discuss the treatment, but not after that. "Remember, it's my mother you're dealing with," Alexandre told the doctor as we were leaving. That was the only time I had tears in my eyes.

I looked for symbols in my routine and religiously followed them. My office was on Fifty-seventh Street and Fifth Avenue, Sloan Kettering on Sixty-eighth Street and the East River, and my apartment at Seventy-sixth Street and Madison Avenue. The route was the shape of a V, so I interpreted it as a V for Victory. Within the V, I found other markers. By walking one block east, then one block

north from my office to the hospital, then walking one block north and one block west on the way home from the hospital, I linked a series of small Vs together within the larger V.

As I walked, I sang a little French victory song I had made up in which the bad cells were killed and never came back. Even now, when I walk fast, the song comes back to me. At the moment of radiation, the second of painless, invisible penetration of the body, I focused on the victorious destruction of the bad cells and the strengthening of the good ones. I used the treatment as a positive tool rather than something I had to surrender to. And I went through it in the best possible way.

The doctors had warned me about me the side effects of the radiation: I would temporarily lose my sense of taste; I would have such a terrible sore throat that I wouldn't be able to swallow; I would lose most of my ability to produce saliva. But my reactions were not as bad as predicted. I didn't lose my saliva, my sense of taste quickly came back, and the pain in my throat was manageable. After the second week, instead of taking the medicine they prescribed for me to anesthetize my throat and help the swallowing, I followed Deepak Chopra's advice to gargle with sesame oil. It worked.

Other sources of help were just as medically unorthodox. Part of my routine on my way home from the hospital soon involved a daily stop at a health food store, where I drank a shot of wheat grass juice. The concentration of enzymes and pure chlorophyll was disgusting, but I believed in its beneficial effects.

I also believed in the massages I had every afternoon. I hadn't realized until I got sick that massages are not about vanity but about helping your immune system. I continue my

weekly shiatsu with Eizo. He gave me a powder of dried GASHU, a rare kind of ginger that healed the blisters in my mouth. I also began meditating for forty minutes twice a day, a regimen I've continued, though reduced now to half an hour or so every morning before I get out of bed. Blocking bad thoughts was helpful. So was my precious healer friend in Paris, Bianca, who has her way of dealing with energies and whom I trust totally. We talked daily over the phone, and she helped me considerably by focusing on positive energy.

Jackie Onassis lost her war with cancer while I was enduring my own, which I found extremely upsetting. I had known Jackie, though not well. I knew she had been sick, and we had shared the same hairdresser, Edgar. Though she was much older than I, I'd admired her for successfully raising her children in the limelight, a challenge I'd also had, though to a much smaller extent. The news of her death was so distressing that for days I refused to read the newspapers or turn on the television. I wanted to feel positive and normal.

I didn't try to cover up the radiation burns on my back and face. In fact, they gave me the look of a good suntan and I convinced myself they were almost becoming, especially on my face, since they emphasized my cheekbones. In the fourth week of radiation, I went to the White House with Mort to a dinner for the emperor and empress of Japan and received many compliments on how well I looked. Perhaps it was the spectacular dress John Galliano lent me, a dress I had seen at his show in Paris that looked like a cloud, it had so many layers of chiffon. It turned out to be the most uncomfortable dress I've ever worn, even though John had sewn an extra piece of fabric onto the bodice for me because the dress, originally made for superthin supermodel Christy

Turlington, was a little tight around the ribs. I added a little more chiffon to the train, which kept falling apart during the dinner, but the dress was so beautiful and glamorous that everyone commented on it, especially the Japanese.

No one questioned why I was a little more tanned on the back than I was on the front. Radiation burns or not, I had not been about to miss going to the White House and meeting the only emperor left in the world. It was an absolutely beautiful night, and my immediate concern as I walked around the Rose Garden was keeping the dress from coming apart.

The doctors at Sloan Kettering were interested in how well I withstood the radiation treatments and asked me to write down what I did. But I found I couldn't. Some would think I was crazy, walking in Vs, talking to a healer over the transatlantic phone line, and soliciting the help of Deepak Chopra. I don't like or believe in gurus, but there are healers who have helped a lot of people who are sick and need assistance to focus on their own energy. There is no question that the mind has a lot of power. To be able to focus on that energy can complement any cure an individual is undertaking. Although meditating and focusing on the mind are not cures, I don't think anyone should underestimate the power and strength we all have within ourselves.

What worked for me might not for others. Each individual reacts differently. One thing I know for sure, however, is how valuable my friends and family were. Though Barry was very involved that summer in planning the merger of QVC and CBS, an idea that ultimately failed, he was there, as always, when I needed him. He lent me his plane on the Fourth of July weekend so that I could take advantage

of the time off from radiation treatment to visit my dying father in Belgium, whom I would never see again. He died three weeks later, just a few days after I finished my treatment. My dear friend Mark Peploe called me daily from the jungles of Malaysia, where he was shooting a movie ironically called *Victory*, and I spoke with my close friend Fred Seidel without fail every night before I went to sleep.

To my great relief, neither my children nor my friends behaved any differently toward me during the treatment, nor did they let on that they were worried. My mother once again was as strong as a rock, keeping her anxiety to herself, which, though it must have been hard on her, made me confident and gave me courage. By acting as if everything were normal and the same, they all allowed me the privacy and the energy to wage and win my own battle.

My brush with cancer made me more compassionate toward other people with sicknesses. And it gave me a new appreciation of life and health, though I thought I'd already had it. It was all so odd, really. I had never been sick before my bout with this disease, I wasn't sick during it, and I haven't been sick since. But it left a lasting impression, adding a new dimension to life itself and the obligation to honor it every day.

When I was a young woman, I thought I'd never make it to thirty. Life was so much fun that I thought I would never get through it. I used to think that I wouldn't live to see the children grow up and, when I bought Cloudwalk, that I would never get to live in it. After age forty, I started to complain about aging like everyone else, but when I was confronted with a life-threatening condition at forty-six, my perspective changed. I went from feeling "Forty-six is so old"

to "Forty-six is so young." Though youth had been so much a part of my identity, I realized that aging gracefully could be as pleasurable. And one opportunity was following on another.

BARRY SOLD HIS STAKE in QVC and soon after took control of the other major shopping channel, Home Shopping Network. I followed him and I was so pleased with the private-label brand deal I had with the network that I wanted to try the same concept with a big retail chain. No designer, to the best of my knowledge, had ever struck such an arrangement with a retailer. My idea was to shorten the distance between the sewing machine and the cash register, which meant cutting out the middleman, lowering the retail price, and sparing me the burden of inventory.

I knew my concept would work only with a retailer whose volume of orders would be large enough to make dealing directly with a manufacturer cost-effective. This effectively cut out the top-tier specialty stores such as Saks, Neiman Marcus, and Nordstrom that ideally I wanted to carry my new brand. I was so determined to avoid the risks and frustrations of inventory, however, that I was willing to compromise. I didn't hesitate, then, when Macy's merged with Federated Department Stores in 1994, bringing the total number of stores to four hundred in thirty-six states.

I could tell from the shine in the eyes of Allen Questrom, the very focused former chairman and CEO of Federated who had orchestrated the big merger with Macy's, that he understood the concept I presented to him over breakfast at New York's Regency Hotel in January 1995. With Federated dealing directly with the suppliers, I pointed

out, the product lines I would design exclusively for him would be competitive with those in successful specialty chains such as Banana Republic, the Gap, and The Limited. Federated would benefit not only by being able to offer the customers an exclusive designer brand at a fabulous price but by having a real live person—me—to promote it.

So Allen was intrigued, and so, in subsequent meetings, was Terry Lundgren, the very attractive chairman of the Federated Merchandising Group, who would move into Allen's job when Allen retired.

At about the same time I had approached Federated, Avon Products and its shining marketing star, Andrea Jung, approached me with an offer I couldn't resist. Avon, which was in the process of expanding its franchise to apparel after 108 years of selling cosmetics and fragrance door-to-door, wanted me to be its first and only designer line.

Avon was relatively down-market, and I initially wasn't quite sure. But because it was a totally different channel of distribution, and Avon made me a concrete offer—a guarantee of $1 million a year plus royalties on anticipated sales of over $40 million—I overcame my doubts and decided to just do it. The day of the announcement, February 2, 1995, Avon stock went up, but the deal raised a few eyebrows at Federated and was eventually one of the main reasons why my negotiations with them collapsed.

In the midst of it all, Alexandre married Alexandra Miller. Alex and Alex, as their friends call them, had known each other for years, well before they were students together at Brown University. Alexandra had grown up in Hong Kong,

where her father, Robert Miller, had overseen his business holdings in Asian duty-free shops, and in New York, where her parents had an apartment two floors above ours. Alexandra loves to tell the story of how she fell in love with Alexandre in the elevator when she was fourteen and he was seventeen. "That's the man I'm going to marry," she decided on the spot.

I was very happy that she proved to be right. Alexandra and her parents, Robert and Chantal, and her older sisters —Pia, who is married to Christopher Getty, and Marie-Chantal, or MC, who is married to Prince Pavlos of Greece —are a loving family. Chantal is a particularly interesting woman, quite shy and reserved, but unquestionably the strength of the family.

I apparently committed a royal faux pas at Pavlos and MC's wedding, which took place in London in 1995 just three months before Alexandre and Alexandra were married in New York. All the kings and queens of the world were in London for the wedding celebration, and Alexandre, along with the future kings of Denmark and Spain, carried the incredibly heavy royal crown of Greece during the Greek Orthodox ceremony. Participating in the ceremony with his royal relatives was an appropriate recognition of his roots. Though Alexandre couldn't understand why he was a prince while he was growing up and thought it meaningless, he carries the name and the title, which go back to the Holy Roman Empire.

My break with protocol came at the wedding luncheon, where I was seated at the same table as King Hussein of Jordan, who was very charming, and Queen Margrethe of Denmark, equally friendly and down-to-earth. My gaffe was

not with them but with the British royal family. I shook hands with Prince Charles and curtsied to Queen Elizabeth, which was appropriate, but the snapshots I took of the queen, which are now in my albums at Cloudwalk, evidently were not. I would read later in a gossip column that no unauthorized person is allowed to photograph the queen. But in all honesty, what mother wouldn't take pictures of her son on the dais two seats away from the queen of England?

His marriage to Alexandra in New York was a little less formal and enormous fun. The only cloud was my mother's health. She had gotten sick a few weeks before the wedding and was so weak and thin that we were all worried that she wasn't going to make it. My mother was on my mind constantly during much of the agitated week I spent around the Millers' dining-room table before the wedding, helping to make seating arrangements for the ball and the luncheon reception. It was Chantal who brilliantly orchestrated it all, starting with the Alexandre Ball on October 26 in two fantastic tents in Battery Park overlooking New York Harbor and ending at a luncheon under two other colorful tents at the old Westbury estate in Long Island.

The huge tents for the Alexandre Ball were designed in an Asian motif by Robert Isabell, the ultimate party planner, who had started his career arranging events at Studio 54. Stepping into the tents was like walking into Shanghai in the 1920s, with groves of bamboos in one tent and a lacquered Chinese pagoda ceiling in the other. During the evening there were amazing fireworks over New York Harbor and, in the tent, acrobats, mimes, and several bands to keep us all dancing until dawn.

The members of the families each hosted their own

tables at the seated dinner for four hundred, and I chose Egon's cousin, Prince Kari Schwartzenberg, as my dinner partner. Kari had been Václav Havel's principal adviser during the Velvet Revolution in Czechoslovakia and is my favorite among Egon's family. Fred Seidel was at the table, too, along with Tina Brown and the painter Francesco Clemente. I was so glad that all my oldest girlfriends—Mireille, Isabel, Nona, Marisa, Florence Grinda, and Irith Landeau—were there to share it with me.

I felt beautiful in a navy blue Saint Laurent couture dress and with my hair done in a seventies style. In a curious way, I realized that I had once again dressed to please Egon. The next night, hundreds of people came to a cocktail party Egon, Tatiana, and I hosted, but we were all very worried about my mother. She was very weak and slightly disoriented during the festivities.

The next morning it was pouring, and I dressed a bit somberly for the wedding. As a matter of fact, Egon remarked that I looked like a Polish matron in my brown dress and with my hair up under a velvet turban. But this was an extraordinary passage for my son, and I didn't want to be conspicuous. Nervous and proud, I escorted Alexandre down the aisle of St. Ignatius Loyola, the same church near our first apartment where, twenty-six years before, I had often stopped to pray for the happiness of the baby I was carrying. Now, fighting back tears, I watched that little blond mischievous boy become a man in front of six hundred people.

Everything about the ceremony was beautiful: the flowers, the music, the decoration of the altar, the mass. The Most Reverend Renato R. Martino, Archbishop of Segerme, performed the ceremony and read a telegram of good wishes

from the pope. Pope John Paul II had been in New York a few weeks before, and Chantal had arranged to have her three daughters and their husbands blessed. Egon and I were very emotional as we left the church together. The sun finally came out during the luncheon and formed a brilliant rainbow over the tent. The atmosphere was so positive that my mother began to look stronger, and eventually she recovered completely. A miracle, once again.

The atmosphere became positive for me as well. Soon after Alexandre's wedding, I went to Paris for the fashion shows. It was there, out of the blue, that Rosemarie Bravo told me she wanted my dresses for Saks. In that instant, every disappointment, every humiliation, every false start I had made since I returned from Paris, was answered. Not only did I regain the professional credibility that remains so important to me, I would succeed in returning my brand to my own identity. My signature is once more my own.

EPILOGUE

As I sit here on this summer Monday morning at Cloudwalk, I cannot help being thankful for so much beauty and happiness. It is a clear day, the birds are singing, the squirrels are running up and down the roof of my studio, the deer are in the orchard eating the apples and peaches. It looks too beautiful to be true.

The book is finished, it will go to production this week and with it will go a lot of anxiety, fear, and some satisfaction. The frustrations of a girl, the life of a woman, the making of a business. It was not an easy task to go back through the journey of it all, the ups and downs, and try to make sense of it, while it is still evolving and changing every day.

I started as a very young girl with an idea. I created a dress, a signature, and I touched an emotional cord in the women who wore that dress. From a dress came a world of other products, bringing a look, an attitude, a spirit of easiness and freedom. As I was learning to be a woman and enjoying being one, I was sharing my discoveries, designing for my needs and making a business out of it. Through the products a dialogue, a connection was created between me and women; I was inspired and I inspired.

The reality of the business world was not easy or

smooth and as I encountered difficulties, I tried to overcome them by making compromises or by taking shortcuts. My goal as I started to work was to obtain independence and freedom. To maintain that independence and freedom I sometimes had to change my path or even quit. There is a price to pay for everything, I learned.

As I grew older, coherence became more and more important to me. I wanted every facet of my life to be a unified reflection of who I was. The books I read, the food I eat, the decors I live in, the friends I have, the causes I choose. As I watched my children grow into adults, I was pleased to see they too had become a reflection of me. They are, I can proudly say, my best work.

But I had had a third child, my brand, and that was no longer an expression of me or my taste. It was crucial to regain control of it and clean it up and restore its integrity, its point of view, its spirit. And I did.

I have tickled the curiosity and the interest of a new generation of young women who have responded with great enthusiasm to the new dresses I designed recently. What a lovely surprise that has been! The best shops from all over the world have ordered the dresses and sold them very well. The demand has been wonderful and very encouraging. I am creating fashion again. I have managed to regain total control of my name for all categories so that I can start clean again: in a new building, with a new look, in a new period, with a new team of qualified and talented people, and, of course, with a beautiful and inspiring young muse, Alexandra. All of this is designed to take the refreshed image into the competitive global marketplace, a very challenging task. Once again I am looking ahead with enthusiasm, hoping to con-

tinue the dialogue I have established with several generations of women through my brand.

When I was little, I dreamed of becoming a certain woman. I became that woman, I would like to remain that woman forever, enjoying life, celebrating it, and inspiring others to do so. I look back and I smile, I look ahead and I smile. Like everyone, I don't like to age, but if each wrinkle is there to remind me of a smile, then wrinkles are not so bad. Life is an adventure and since I love it with a passion, I try to respect it and honor it every day, no matter how difficult it sometimes can be. I find strength in loving my family and my friends, who make the fabric of my life, but also and always in exploring new roads and new landscapes. And, as in nature, what I find most reassuring and inspiring is that it is never still.

DVF

July 1998